Perspectives on Teacher Education

R.P. Pathak

ATLANTIC

PUBLISHERS & DISTRIBUTORS (P) LTD

Published by

ATLANTIC

PUBLISHERS & DISTRIBUTORS (P) LTD

7/22, Ansari Road, Darya Ganj, New Delhi-110002
Phones : +91-11-40775252, 40775214, 23273880, 23275880
Fax : +91-11-23285873
Web : www.atlanticbooks.com
E-mail : orders@atlanticbooks.com

Branch Office: Chennai
Phones : +91-44-48531784, 28291383
E-mail : chennai@atlanticbooks.com

Printed & bound in India by Atlantic Print Services

Preface

Education is the foundation stone of a nation's intellectual competence which shapes the power profile of a nation in the comity of nations. Thus, it is rightly said that the progress of a country, particularly of a democratic country, depends upon the quality of teachers and of its system of education, and for this reason, teaching is considered the noblest among all professions.

Teachers have always played a crucial role in preparing communities and societies towards exploring new horizons of knowledge and achieving higher levels of progress and development. They are the prime agents of change. The significance of the emerging role of teachers has never been so critical as at this juncture. Teacher education is an age-old concept, but it has been undergoing transformations over the years and assuming new meanings and dimensions due to changes in socio-cultural and political conditions of the society.

Teaching is one of the oldest and most respected professions; and the roles, functions, and preparation of teachers undergo changes from time to time. Teacher education is both pre-service and in-service. The question of duration, content, and methodology has attracted the attention of educationists from time to time. There are various agencies to evolve a comprehensive and systematic organisational framework for in-service education and training of teachers, like National Council of Educational Research and Training (NCERT), National University of Educational Planning and Administration (NUEPA), State Council of Educational Research and Training (SCERT), District Institute of Education and Training (DIET), and many others. They help in extending the disciplines in behavioural science through training and research.

Several commissions and committees have reviewed the achievements and made recommendations in the field of education in general and teacher education in particular. It has been felt that teacher education is a critical area in which adequate inputs and investments are to be made for developing not only human resources but also physical resources.

The subject matter of this book has been divided into 10 chapters which take up all the major aspects and issues of teacher education. It will be a useful text for the students of B.Ed., M.Ed., and those pursuing M.Phil. and Ph.D. It will also help educationalists and all those connected with teacher education in India.

I wish to thank my colleagues in different institutions and various authors whose works I have consulted in writing this book. Many people have contributed directly or indirectly in the preparation of this book, and I convey my thanks to all. I also thank Dr. Tamanna Kaushal for final shaping of the book. I am also obliged to the entire team of Atlantic Publishers and Distributors, New Delhi, for publishing this book.

Any valuable suggestion for the improvement of the book is most welcome.

R.P. Pathak

Contents

Chapter 1

Aims and Objectives of Teacher Education

STRUCTURE OF CHAPTER

INTRODUCTION

Changes are taking place in all the aspects of our life. In the realm of education, objectives, content and process, all the stages are undergoing change. These changes are emanating from socio-economic evolution taking place in the country, explosion of knowledge, advances in pedagogical science, revision of school curricula, etc. This situation demands suitable changes in the curricula of teacher education at different stages. These changes also reflect an imperative need for education of teachers to prepare them for realization of the changing objectives of school education. The need for in-service education of teachers is also now being greatly realized today. These aspects of the teacher education have been discussed in detail in this chapter.

NEED FOR EDUCATION OF TEACHERS

Until recently, teaching was considered as only an art. It was therefore believed that those who possess this art can only become successful teachers. It was further believed that this talent/art of teaching is an innate ability and no training can develop this in an individual. The training to prepare teachers was therefore, not considered essential.

Teaching is now considered not only as an art but as a science too. It is now being increasingly realised that the ability to teach can be developed in an individual. The talent of those who have this innate talent, can further be improved through a well-designed programme of teacher education. This is based on the premise that teaching can be studied objectively, and successful instructional approaches and strategies can be identified and developed through a well-designed programme. Allen and Ryan (USA) and B.K. Passi, N.K. Jangira and L.C. Singh (India) have analysed the teaching act into teaching skills and have successfully demonstrated through a number of research studies that teaching competence and skills can be developed/improved among prospective and in-service teachers.

We would understand the need of education for teachers if we consider the role of a teacher precisely. He is to foster an all-round development of children under his care. For this purpose, it is very essential for him to understand the process of development of children. He needs to understand the objectives of school education in general and of the stage of education with which he is working. He is required to inculcate desired values among children in order to strengthen democratic and secular fabric of our society. He needs training to acquire successful strategies of inculcating values. He is to deal with pupils of diverse abilities. He is to conduct action research to solve their concerns and to undertake continuous and comprehensive evaluation of the pupils. He is to extend the needed support to the community and seek their support for effective functioning of his school. For performing all these roles, he needs to acquire the required skills and competencies which can only be developed through a teacher education programme.

GENERAL AIMS AND OBJECTIVES OF TEACHER EDUCATION

As we are aware, a teacher has the prime responsibility of fostering an all-round development of the children under his wings. He purposes them to become good citizens, who profess and keep faith in the democratic, secular and socialistic values. In accordance with this, his education and training should instill the same values and skills in him.

General Aim

A teacher needs to be appropriately equipped to have a vision of the emerging social order, so that he is able to prepare his children for the same. A prospective teacher, in addition of acquiring professional knowledge and skills, should also attain the necessary attitudes which would enable him to play his role effectively in bringing about the desired changes in pupils through education.

The foregoing paragraphs would have convinced you that the objectives of a teacher education programme can never be static. These should undergo changes from time to time in accordance with the technological development of a society, changes in school curricula as a result of explosion in knowledge, socio-political changes in that country, etc. In India, objectives of teacher education programme have therefore been revised from time to time.

The document entitled 'Teacher Education Curriculum: A Framework—1978' NCTE brought out by the National Council for Teacher Education suggests a set of twelve broad objectives of teacher education programmes in general, followed by objectives of teacher education at different levels. Programmes of teacher education are designed by different universities for their affiliated colleges of education. Though these programmes differ from university to university, the objectives of these programmes are more or less the same. The department of Teacher Education and Special Education of the NCERT, revised in 1991 the curriculum of teacher education for both the stages (elementary and secondary). The objectives of these programmes are mentioned briefly mentioned below:

Aim and Objectives of Teacher Education

The objectives of curricula for different stages of teacher education are somewhat different. The general objectives of teacher education are to:

- Develop an understanding of the objectives of school education in the Indian context.
- Develop interests, attitudes, and skills which would enable them to foster an all-round growth and development of children under their care.
- Develop competence to teach through learner-centred approach.
- Help them to acquire teaching skills and strategies for facilitating optimum learning on pupils' part.
- Develop an understanding of the process of development of children.
- Develop an understanding of the needs, tasks, and problems of children for the development of a well-integrated and balanced personality.
- Develop capabilities of organising co-curricular activities.
- Develop capabilities to perceive problems and conduct action research.
- Develop an awareness of professional ethics.
- Acquire experiences in conducting continuous and comprehensive evaluation.
- Help them to precisely perceive the role of education in national development.
- Develop an understanding of the multidimensional nature of society's role as a catalytic agent in the society.
- Develop an understanding of the role and functions of a teacher as envisaged in the emerging Indian society.

- Develop a warm and positive attitude towards growing children and their academic socio-emotional personal problems, etc.
- Develop skills to involve community in optimum functioning of school.
- Develop competence to integrate core elements of the national curriculum with teaching of different subjects.

Evaluate Yourself

1. Given below are multiple choice objective questions. Please put a tick (✓) against correct response.

(i) There is a need for a teacher education programme because:

(a) Teaching is an art.

(b) Teaching is a science.

(c) Teaching is an art as well as science.

(d) Teaching is neither a science nor an art.

(ii) Teacher education programme is needed because:

(a) A teacher is to deal with pupils of both the sexes.

(b) A teacher is to teach in a number of periods daily.

(c) A teacher is to deal with children of diverse abilities.

(d) A teacher is to learn how to respect the principal of the school.

(iii) The main role of a teacher is to:

(a) Develop communication skill among pupils.

(b) Foster an all-round development of pupils.

(c) To facilitate pupils' cognitive development.

(d) To promote pupils' physical development.

(iv) The programme of teacher education is essential:

(a) To inculcate desired values among prospective teachers.

(b) Not only to inculcate desired values among prospective teachers, but to also help them to acquire strategies which they can inculcate among pupils.

(c) Inculcation of values is not the responsibility of a secondary teacher.

(d) Inculcation of values is the responsibilities of an elementary teacher only.

TYPES AND PURPOSES OF TEACHER EDUCATION

Teacher education is broadly classified into the following two types:

- Pre-service Teacher Education
- In-service Teacher Education

Pre-service Teacher Education

Pre-service teacher education stands for the programme which is designed to prepare teachers. Different programmes are designed for different levels of school education—pre-school, elementary, and secondary education. The teacher education programmes for these levels of school education are as follows:

1. Pre-school Teacher Education
2. Elementary Teacher Education
3. Secondary Teacher Education

1. *Pre-school Teacher Education*

Pre-school teacher education refers to teacher education programme which is designed to prepare teachers for pre-school classes—Nursery, Kindergarden, etc. The duration of this course is mostly one year. In India, the central as well as the state governments are yet to accept the responsibility of preparing teachers for pre-school classes. As such, most of the Nursery teacher training institutions are run by non-government bodies. However, in Delhi, one Nursery teacher training institution at Darya Ganj is run by Delhi Administration. The duration of this course is two years. The minimum qualifications for admission into these institutions is generally 10+2. One of the departments of the National Institute of Education, NCERT, Delhi, Department of Pre-school and Elementary education, guides Nursery teacher training institutions in the development of appropriate syllabi for different classes and the transactional approaches which teachers should adopt in dealing with kids.

2. *Elementary Teacher Education*

Elementary Teacher Education is a programme designed to prepare teachers for classes I to VIII. In some states, however, these teachers are required to teach only the primary classes, that is, I to V. The duration of this course is two years in most of the states. In some states like Andhra Pradesh and Manipur, the duration of the programme is one year. Elementary teacher training institutions located in different states offer this course, Quite recently, District Institutes of Education and Training (DIETs) set up by the Ministry of Human Resource Development have also started offering the course. The minimum qualifications for admission into an elementary teacher training institution/DIET is 10+2. The certificate/diploma in Education is awarded by the Education Department/State Board of School Education of the state in which the institution is located.

3. *Secondary Teacher Education*

Secondary teacher education programme is organised by secondary colleges of education affiliated to different universities. The duration of this course is one year. In some states, departments of education of the universities also offer the programme. The purpose of the secondary teacher education programme is to prepare teachers for classes IX to XII. The degree i.e. Bachelor in Education is awarded by the university to which a secondary college of education is affiliated. The minimum qualifications for admission into secondary colleges of education is Bachelor Degree in Arts/Science. Four Regional Institute of Education located at Ajmer, Bhopal, Bhubaneshwar, and Mysore are however, offering four-year integrated courses leading to degree such as B.Sc. B.Ed./B.A. B.Ed. The minimum qualifications for admission into the four-year integrated course is 10+2.

In-service Teacher Education

We may be working as a teacher and have experience of teaching in a school and would know that education is a continuous process. No formal pre-service education in a college/ university and/or college of education can fully prepare a person to discharge his professional responsibilities effectively forever.

At best, it can help him to acquire the existing knowledge and skills and instill in him an attitude, which would cause him to seek new knowledge and skills as he progresses in his professional career. Without this attitude, a professional would generally be ineffective in performing his professional responsibilities.

Changes in school curriculum as a result of explosion of knowledge, advances in pedagogical science, changing social needs, and demands require teachers to acquire new knowledge and skills, modify their attitudes and interests to cope with the changing needs and demands of society. Thus, the importance of in-service education to help teachers to acquire new concepts, skills, etc. hardly needs any emphasis.

"The further training of teachers in service works like a tonic, like an injection that helps to protect the body from different diseases, and the commonest disease teachers suffer from is arteriosclerosis, that is long set habits that become a second nature forcing them to act always in the old well-established way, independently of the transformed world around them." (Levin, 1962).

The National Commission on Teacher Education (1985) NCT also highlighted that 'with the explosion of knowledge, revolution in the world of media with contemporary issues, demanding urgent attention with values getting eroded, the need for helping teachers to keep barest of things cannot be questioned'. All the above points prove the need for in-service education of the teachers.

ORGANISATION OF IN-SERVICE PROGRAMMES

Until quite recently, the State Institutes of Education (SIE)/ State Institutes of Science Education (SISE)/State Institute of Educational Technology/State Councils of Education Research and Training, were the only institutions which were organising in-service programmes for teachers. Since the number of teachers working at the elementary, secondary, and senior secondary levels has increased substantially, these institutions were not able to provide training to teachers periodically. The Ministry of Human Resources and Development (MHRD) has therefore, created other institutions—District Institutes of Education and

Training (DIETs), Institutes of Advanced Studies in Education (IASEs), and strengthening Colleges of Teacher Education (CTEs) for in-service education of teachers.

The District Institutes of Education and Training (DIETs) have been given the responsibility to provide in-service education to primary and upper primary teachers periodically. The number of DIETs proposed to be set up is four hundred. Of these, more than three hundred have already been set up in different parts of the country. The remaining are to be set up during the current Eight Five Year Plan.

Institute of Advanced Studies in Education (IASE) has been given the responsibility to provide in-service education to senior secondary teachers. The number of IASEs proposed to be set up is fifty in the country. Of these fifty IASEs, only a limited number have been created so far. CTEs are to provide in-service education to secondary teachers. The number of CTEs proposed to set up is two hundred. Of these, very limited number have been set up so far.

With the creation of said institutes—DIETs, IASEs, and CTEs, the facilities for in-service education of teachers have increased substantially. It may contribute a lot towards qualitative improvement of education at the levels—elementary, secondary, and senior secondary.

Evaluate Yourself

2. Fill in the blanks in the following statements.

(i) The teacher education is broadly classified into two categories .... and ....

(ii) There are .... levels of teacher education programmes.

(iii) The levels of teacher education programme are ....
....

(iv) The purpose of pre-service teacher education is to ....

(v) Secondary teacher education programme is organised by ....

(vi) The word DIET stands for ....

(vii) The pre-service programme for preparing elementary teachers is organised by ....

(viii) The number of DIETs proposed to be set up in the country is ....

(ix) The number of CTEs and IASEs proposed to be set up are .... and .... respectively.

(x) The responsibility of providing in-service education to secondary school teachers rests on ....

(xi) District Institutes of Education and Training are required to provide in-service education to .... and ....

(xii) In-service education to senior secondary school teachers is required to be provided by ....

(xiii) According to Levin, the commonest disease from which teachers suffer is ....

(xiv) The purpose of DIETs is to prepare teachers to teach classes from .... to ....

(xv) In-service education of teacher is essential to ....

SUMMARY

1. Until recently, the need for education of teachers was not considered necessary as teaching was considered as only an art.
2. It is now being realised that teaching is science as well.
3. Teaching skills, instructional approaches, and strategies can be identified and training can be provided to equip individuals with these.
4. Further, the need for education of teachers is essential as teachers—in addition to teaching—are required to perform other roles, such as, inculcation of values, undertake continuous and comprehensive evaluation, interact with the community for seeking support for better functioning of the school, etc.

5. The teacher is also to deal with pupils of diverse abilities and in different settings—large classes, multi-grade teaching, etc.
6. In view of these roles, the education of teachers is highly essential to develop the requisite skills and competencies.
7. The main objectives of a teacher education programme is to help prospective teachers understand the process of development of children, their learning process, develop warm and positive attitude towards them and to acquire requisite skills, strategies and competencies to bring about an all-round development of children under their care.
8. Teacher education is broadly classified into two types—pre-service and in-service teacher education.
9. There are three levels of pre-service teacher education programme such as pre-school teacher education, elementary teacher education, and secondary teacher education.
10. Whereas the purpose of pre-service teacher education is to prepare teachers, the purpose of in-service teacher education is to update the teacher's knowledge in different subjects, improve their teaching skills, equip them with latest teaching strategies, etc.
11. In-service education to primary and upper primary teachers is now provided by the District Institutes Education and Training.
12. Training of Senior Secondary and secondary teachers is to be taken care of by IASEs and CTEs respectively.

MODEL ANSWERS

1. (i) c, (ii) c, (iii) b, (iv) b, (v) a, (vi) b, (vii) b
2. (i) Pre-service and In-service
   (ii) Two
   (iii) Pre-school teacher education, Elementary and Secondary teacher education

(iv) Prepare teachers
(v) Colleges of education and University departments of education.
(vi) District Institute of Education and Training
(vii) DIETs and ETTIs
(viii) 400
(ix) 200 and 50
(x) CTEs
(xi) Primary and upper primary school teachers
(xii) IASEs
(xiii) Arteriosclerosis
(xiv) I to VIII
(xv) Improve the quality of education in schools.

KEYWORDS

Pre-school Education: Stands for classes Nursery, K.G., etc.

Elementary Education: Primary education stands for classes I to V. Upper primary education stands for classes VI to VIII. Elementary Education stands for classes I to VIII.

Secondary Education: Stands for classes IX and X.

Senior Secondary Education: Stands for classes XI and XII.

REFERENCES

Bhattacharya, G.S. (1990). *Teacher Education*, Agra, Vinod Pustak Mandir.

Levin, S. (1962). *The Further Training of Teachers in Service*. International Federation of Teachers' Association (Mimeo).

Moffit, John Clifton (1983). *In-service Education for Teachers*, Washington: The Centre for Applied Research in Education Inc.

NCERT (1990). *Elementary Teacher Education Curriculum—Guidelines and Syllabi*, New Delhi.

NCERT (1990). *Secondary Teacher Education Curriculum—Guidelines and Syllabi*, New Delhi.

Saxena, N.R. (1988). *Teacher Education*, Meerut, R. Lall Book Depot.

Singh, L.C. (1990). (Ed.) *Teacher Education in India—A Resource Book*, New Delhi, NCERT.

FURTHER READINGS

Gupta, A.K. (1988). *Teacher Education*, Sterling Publishers, New Delhi.

Green, T.F. (1971). *The Activities of Teaching*, McGraw Hill Book Co., New York.

Jangira, N.K. (1979). *Teacher's Training and Teacher's*. Effectiveness, National Publishing House, New Delhi.

Sharma, R.A. (1986). *Teacher Education*, Meerut, International Publishing House.

Shukla, R.S. (1978). *Emerging Trends in Teacher Education*, Allahabad, Chug Publication.

Chapter 2

Curriculum of Teacher Education

STRUCTURE OF CHAPTER

We have studied the need for education of teachers and the objectives of teacher education programme. Besides, we have studied the types of teacher education programmes. In this chapter, we would study the curriculum of teacher education programme and the principles involved in formulating the same.

In addition to this, a critical appraisal of B.Ed./M.Ed. syllabi of some Indian Universities is presented.

INTRODUCTION

There is a linkage between the educational policy, school curriculum, and the teacher education curriculum. The educational policy of a state influences the school curriculum. On the other hand, the formulation of teacher education curriculum is influenced by both the school curriculum and the educational policy of the state. The teacher education curriculum therefore, needs to be designed in such a way that it becomes an effective instrument for the implementation of the state educational policy.

There are mainly two major components of a teacher education programme—theory aspect and practice of teaching. Both of these aspects need to be designed to prepare prospective teachers to transact the school curriculum effectively, and realise the objectives of school education. We would learn about these components in details in this chapter.

COMPONENTS OF TEACHER EDUCATION CURRICULUM

Each university in the country develops curricula for various courses of teacher education—B.Ed., M.Ed., and M.Phill. (Education). These curricula therefore, differ from one university the other. We are aware that these curricula developed by universities are implemented by colleges of education affiliated to the university concerned. Most university departments of education offer only M.Ed. and M.Phil. (Education) programmes. In some states, some affiliated colleges of education also offer M.Ed. programme in addition to B.Ed. programme.

We know the courses which constitute a B.Ed. programme. Given below are the current courses which generally constitute a B.Ed. programme. These may be the same or somewhat different from the courses which we were offered when we were a B.Ed. student.

- Principles of Education in the Emerging Indian Society
- Educational Psychology

- General Methods of Teaching/Content-cum-Methodology
- Methods of Teaching School Subjects—English/Hindi/Sanskrit/Physical Science/Biological Sciences/Maths/Social Studies, etc.
- Current Problems in Indian Education
- Working with the community

The following courses generally constitute a M.Ed. programme. These courses may be different from those which were offered in your M.Ed. programme. This is because these courses differ from university to university.

- Philosophical and Sociological Foundations of Education
- Advanced Educational Psychology
- Methods of Research
- Optional papers:
  (a) Educational and Vocational Guidance
  (b) Teacher Education
  (c) Mental Hygiene, etc.

The curriculum for elementary teacher education is developed by State Boards of Secondary Education/State Department of Education. The curriculum, therefore, differs from state to state. These courses are offered by the elementary teacher training institutions. Recently, the Ministry of Human Resource Department (MHRD) has set up District Institutes of Education and Training (DIETs), which are offering the said course and preparing teachers to teach elementary classes. The curriculum at this stage generally constitutes the following courses:

- Teacher Education in the Emerging Indian Society.
- Child Psychology
- Principles and Problems of Elementary Education
- Working with the community
- Content-cum-Methodology and Practice
- Teaching and Related Practical Work

The Curriculum for different courses for teacher education programme is revised from time to time. The revision is necessitated due to changes in objectives of school education and in content and process of school curricula, as a result of explosion of knowledge, advances in pedagogical science, stage of technological development in the country, socio-political changes, etc. The National Policy on Education (1986) suggested an overhauling of teacher education curriculum. In pursuance of the policy, the Department of Teacher Education, revised in 1991, the curriculum for teacher education, both at the elementary and secondary levels, keeping in view major thrusts of the National Policy on Education (1986). The following are the main components of the curriculum, both at the elementary and secondary levels.

- Foundation Course
- Stage Relevant Specialization
- Additional Specialization
- Practicum/Field work

Foundation Course

The objective of the foundation course is to provide the student teachers with necessary theoretical insights into the understanding of aims and objectives of education in the context of national development with reference to socio-cultural, political, and economic imperatives. Besides, these student teachers are to develop an understanding of the process of human development and learning. The following two courses constitute this component:

- Education in the Emerging India (Philosophical and social-cultural perspectives)
- Educational Psychology (with focus on learners' development and stage, learning adjustment)

Stage Relevant Specialization

This component includes historical background and scope of education at the stage concerned and functions of a teacher with reference to curriculum planning strategies, teaching skills, evaluation, management, guidance and counselling, co-curricular activities, etc. This component comprises of the following course at the B.Ed. level:

- Stage of School Education and Teacher Functions
- Specialization in the methodology of
    (i) A secondary school subject with prior specialization
    (ii) A secondary/senior secondary/primary school subject.

In case of teacher education at the elementary stage, the stage-relevant specialization consists of the following:

- Elementary Education and Teacher Functions
- Language Teaching (Mother Tongue and English)
- Mathematics Teaching
- Environment Studies Teaching (as related to standards I to V)
- Health and Physical Education
- Art Education
- Work-experience

Additional Specialization

The teacher of modern times is required to play multiple roles. Besides teaching normal children, he is to teach children with disability. He is to provide guidance and counselling to pupils. He is also expected to conduct action research, etc., to seek solution to the problems faced by him. In view of these roles, students and teachers at the secondary and elementary levels, need to have specialization in one of the following areas:

Adult Education	– Library Services
Distance Education	– Work Experience
Special Education	– Educational and Vocational Guidance
Computer Application	– Non-formal Education
Educational Technology	– Health and Physical Education
Secondary Education	– Art Education
Tribal Education	– Action Research

Practicum/Field Work

This component consists of the following three aspects:

(i) School Experience Programme (SEP)

(ii) Practical work including working with community, social service, and work-experience

(iii) Time Allocation of Curriculum Components

School Experience Programme (SEP)

Generally in our College of Education, students and teachers are provided experiences only to learn how to teach. They are sent to practising schools where they teach a fixed number of lessons. This aspect of training is known as practice-teaching programme. The term 'School Experience Programme' emphasizes that besides providing experiences for learning to teach, prospective teachers also need to learn how to perform other roles expected of them, outside the classroom and within the school. These provide them a broader vision and perspectives of their roles and functions in the total school programme. Thus the term SEP is wider in scope than the practice-teaching programme.

Practical Work including Working with Community and Social Service

The major purpose of this component is to provide suitable experiences to prospective teachers so that they acquire the requisite skills and competencies, which would help them to work with the community for mutual benefit and also to do social service.

Work experience is another component under the practical work. The purpose of this component is to provide experiences to students and teachers for purposive and meaningful manual work, resulting in either goods or services useful to community. Student teachers should therefore, acquire the necessary skills and competencies for planning, organizing, performing, and evaluating work experience activities laid down for school children.

Time Allocation of Curriculum Components

The weightage in terms of time, to be devoted for different courses in secondary colleges of education, is given below:

Curriculum Component	Weightage in terms of time
(a) Foundation Course	20%
(i) Education in the Emerging Indian (10%)	
(ii) Educational Psychology (10%)	
(b) Stage Relevant Specialization	30%
(iii) Secondary Education & Teacher functions (10%)	
(iv) Specialization in Methodology of a Secondary School Subject with Prior Specialization (10%)	
(v) A secondary/Higher Secondary/Primary school subject (10%)	
(c) Additional Specialisation	10%
(vi) An elective from the area such as Adult Education Population Education, Distance Education, Special Education, Tribal Education, etc.	
(d) Practicum/Field Work	40%
(vii) Internship in teaching including field assignments (20%)	
(viii) Practical work including work experience, working with the community, social service (20%)	

The time allocation for different components of the curriculum at the elementary level is almost the same as that for secondary level.

The teacher education curriculum developed by NCERT, both for secondary and elementary levels, is an illustration of the recently revised curriculum. Different Universities/State

Boards of School Education are likely to revise their curricula for secondary and elementary level teacher education, by adopting/ adapting the same in near future. The University of Dibrugarh has recently revised their curriculum of B.Ed. Programme on the lines of NCERT and NCTE Curriculum. SCERT, Delhi and Punjab have also recently revised their curriculum for elementary teacher education on the lines of the curriculum developed by the NCERT and NCTE.

Evaluate Yourself

1. Mention three reasons necessitating revision of teacher education curriculum at the B.Ed. level from time to time.
2. Mention one area of additional specialization which is essential for promoting education of adult.
3. Differentiate between concepts of school experience programme and the teaching practice programme.

PLACE OF GENERAL EDUCATION IN THE TEACHER EDUCATION CURRICULUM

We also know that in the one-year B.Ed. Programme, a great emphasis is laid on teaching of foundation courses, which includes Education in the Emerging India and Educational Psychology, Teacher functions, Teaching of two school subjects, one additional specialization and Practicum and Field work. Therefore, general education does not find place in the teacher education curriculum at the secondary level.

However, the position is different in the four-year integrated course of teacher education, being organised by the Regional Institute of Education of NCERT. These courses lead to degree, i.e. B.Sc. B.Ed., B.A. B.Ed. and B.Com. B.Ed. In these programmes, general education is taught in all the years of the course along with professional education. The duration of the elementary teacher education programme is two years in most of the states but in states like Andhra Pradesh, Manipur, the duration of the course is still one year. Where the programme of elementary teacher education is two years, the enrichment of school education content is an important component of the programme. This is because the minimum qualification for admission into an elementary teacher training institution/ District Institute of Education and Training is 10+2 in most of the states and union territories. Enrichment of school content in teacher education programme is, therefore, quite needed and desirable.

PRINCIPLES AND OBJECTIVES OF ORGANIZATION OF TEACHING PRACTICE PROGRAMME

Practice teaching is the most important component of the teacher education programme. The purpose of this component is to provide experience to prospective teachers to equip them with teaching skills and strategies so that they acquire the competencies to teach effectively in the classroom. The specific objectives of teaching practice programme are to:

- acquaint prospective teachers with the condition under which they will be normally required to work after becoming teachers
- have a feel of problems which teachers face in the real school situations and possible ways of dealing with them
- plan and prepare lessons of different subjects required to be taught
- acquire a number of teaching skills such as writing instructional objectives, selecting and organising learning material, development and using teaching aids, increasing pupil's participation, diagnosing pupils' progress, closure, etc.
- try out different teaching strategies
- develop competence to make use of learned centred approach
- proper use of communication media (print and non-print in a variety of situations)
- acquire skills in identifying children having special needs and understanding their behaviours
- develop skills for seeking community support for the school

- develop skills for organising co-curriculum activities, etc.
- learn to deal with first generation learners
- acquire competence to teach in a variety of settings
- prepare attendance and fee register
- construct achievement test
- maintaining cumulative record of pupils, etc.

It is evident from the list of objectives mentioned above that the practice-teaching programme is designed to provide experience of varied nature to prospective teachers.

In many colleges of education, both at the elementary and secondary levels, the requisite teaching skills and strategies are developed through micro-teaching approach. After acquiring skills and strategies, students and teachers are sent to practising schools to teach in real classroom settings.

Evaluate Yourself

1. Justify in five sentences the need of general education in elementary teacher education programme.
2. Mention five main objectives of practice-teaching programme.

CRITICAL APPRAISAL OF B.ED./M.ED. SYLLABI OF SOME INDIAN UNIVERSITIES

It has already been mentioned in the foregoing pages that each university develops its own curricula of B.Ed./M.Ed. programme. A review of syllabi of these courses of different universities reveals the weaknesses which are mentioned below:

- Curricula are outdated.
- Methods of teaching mentioned in these syllabi have very limited use and applicability in classroom settings.
- Vitality and realism are lacking in these curricula.
- Set patterns of lesson planning and rigid techniques of teaching are followed in practice-teaching programme.
- These curricula provide the students/teachers very little awareness of the role that the education can play in

transforming the present Indian society into a truly democratic, socialistic, and secular society.

- Advances in pedagogical science are not reflected in these curricula.
- Curricula provide a little or no importance to action research projects to be conducted by B.Ed./M.Ed. students.
- Very little emphasis is laid upon inculcation of desirable values and fostering positive attitudes towards the teaching profession among students/teachers.
- Development of scientific temper among prospective teachers is hardly an objective.
- Adequate experiences to manage learning in variety of settings—multi-grade teaching, large classes, etc. are not provided.
- Curriculum do not make provision for experiences for working with community, micro planning and school mapping, etc.
- Curricula do not envisage experiences to integrate the core elements mentioned in the NPE (1986) with teaching of content in different subjects.

Curricula at the B.Ed./M.Ed. Level do not reflect changing role of the teacher in the emerging Indian society.

Curricula do not reflect the significant contribution made by Piaget and Bruner in the area of cognitive development and concept attainment process respectively.

Curricula do not envisage developing of skills for identifying children with learning disabilities.

Activity 1

The list of weaknesses in the existing curricula of B.Ed. and M.Ed. programmes is not exhaustive. We have already done B.Ed. Mention the additional weaknesses which we identified when we were undergoing experiences in the B.Ed. course.

PRINCIPLES OF FORMULATING THE CURRICULAR AND CO-CURRICULAR PROGRAMMES

Formulation of curriculum is a scientific process. It clearly specifies the content to be converted and the learning experiences to be provided to trainees. A well-organised curriculum is of immense value to both teachers and the taught. It should therefore, reflect the functional utility. Logical and functional relationships among various aspects of the curriculum are also very essential. The curriculum planner endeavours to realise the objectives of the programme through the content which constitutes the curriculum and the process of transacting the same.

Principles of Formulating Curricular Programmes

This process of formulating curricular programmes involves certain principles, which are mentioned below in brief:

Principle of Relevance

One of the most important principles of developing curricular programmes of teacher education is its relevance to the responsibilities that prospective teachers are expected to discharge after they become teachers. Teachers are required to teach; promote physical, emotional and cognitive development of pupils; inculcate values, interact with the community to seek their support for the school and extend support to the community for their benefit; and conduct action research to solve their problems in a scientific way. Teacher education curriculum, to be relevant, needs to be designed to equip teachers with desirable understanding and skills, so that they are able to discharge their responsibilities effectively inside and outside the classroom.

Principles of Utility

Another principle of formulating the curriculum is its functional utility. We have already completed B.Ed. course. Now we may be knowing that many topics in different courses taught to we are not of any utility to we when we are functioning as a teacher in our school. On the contrary, there are certain topics such as Piaget's theory of cognitive development and the principles of teaching learning, which are of immense value to teachers, but do not find a place in educational psychology course in B.Ed. curriculum of most of the universities. The formulation of curricular programme therefore, needs to be based on the principles of utility.

Principle of Variety

The principle of variety is another principle which should guide the formulation of the curriculum of teacher education. A class of today is heterogeneous in nature as regards the interests, needs and aspirations of students who constitute it. The school should therefore, make provision for a variety of experiences satisfying the varying needs and interests of pupils. The teacher education curriculum at different levels should provide a variety of experiences to student teachers, suiting to their capabilities and needs.

Principle of Flexibility

A rigid curriculum at either school level or teacher education level is of limited value. This is because the objectives of school education undergo change from time to time in the light of emerging social needs, expectations, explosion of knowledge, and technological advancement of the country, etc. As such, planners of teacher education curriculum should build a certain amount of flexibility into the curriculum and in its transaction. For instance, different colleges of education located in different parts of the country should have the freedom to modify certain aspects of the curriculum in light of their local specific needs.

The said principles are some of the most important ones for formulating curricular programmes.

Principles of Organisation Co-curricular Activities

It is now universally accepted that education cannot be provided to pupils only through the curricular programmes. Co-curricular activities can also be used effectively in a school to impart the requisite knowledge and provide necessary training.

The following are some of the co-curricular activities which are generally organised in schools:

- Literary activities—debates, symposia, panel discussions, mock parliament, poetry reading, bringing out monthly and annual magazines, bulletins, etc.
- Celebration of festivals of national and international days and anniversaries of great men
- Music, dramas, and dance
- Mock courts
- Hobby clubs
- Games and sports
- Excursions—visits to educational institutions, picnics, etc.

There are a number of principles which need to be followed in organising co-curricular programmes. It should supplement curricular programmes in providing the requisite knowledge to teacher trainees. Secondly, these programmes should provide experiences to trainees to develop their talent in certain fields such as, dancing, creative thinking, music, dramas, etc. Thirdly, co-curricular activities need to be organised in such a way that they promote social qualities such as, co-operation, tolerance, etc. They should also promote National integration and preservation of cultural heritage. Another principle of organising their programmes is to provide adequate and suitable experiences to student teachers so that they acquire the requisite capability to organise these activities in school.

Evaluate Yourself

1. Mention the principles of formulating curricular programmes.
2. Mention five co-curricular activities which are generally organised in secondary schools.
3. Mention the purposes for which co-curricular programmes need to be organised in training colleges.

FUNCTIONAL APPROACH TO TEACHER EDUCATION CURRICULUM

It is widely accepted that teacher education curricula of most of the universities are quite outdated. These are of limited utility in preparing prospective teachers to discharge their responsibilities effectively, when they become teachers. Many topics in certain courses taught in teacher education programme are of little relevance to practitioners in schools. Hence, these is a need to make teacher education programmes more functional.

Studies need to be conducted to analyse the tasks of teaching in different contexts—multi-grade teaching, large classes, children from tribal areas, children with different disabilities, first generation learners, etc. Education teacher curriculum needs to be developed, taking into consideration the tasks to be performed by teachers in different contexts and conditions. Skills required to perform various tasks may be identified. Prospective teachers may be provided training through micro-teaching approach to acquire the requisite skills.

Besides acquisition of skills, prospective teachers may be equipped with latest teaching strategies such as, Learner Centred Approach, Inquiring Training Model, Concept Attainment Model, Advance Organiser Model, Biological Science Inquiry Model, etc.

Presently, the teaching practice programme is very limited in scope. It needs to be replaced by internship in teaching or School Experience Programme (SEP). Student teachers need to be attached to schools for a specified period like one month or so. They need to be provided experience to perform all the tasks that the regular teachers do. This would go a long way in preparing better teachers for tomorrow.

The said suggestions if implemented would, make the existing teacher education programme more functional.

SUMMARY

1. In this chapter, we have studied the main components of teacher education curriculum, both at the elementary and secondary levels.
2. There are four main components of a teacher education curriculum—Foundation Courses, Stage Relevant Specialization, Additional Specialization and Practicum/ Field work.

3. Foundation component constitutes two courses—Education in the Emerging India and Educational Psychology.
4. The second component constitutes courses—Stage of school education and Teacher functions, and Specialization in the methodology of teaching subjects.
5. The component of additional specialization Stands for various courses such as Adult education, Special education, Computer application, Tribal education, Non-formal education, etc.
6. A student teacher is to select one out of such courses.
7. The further component relates to Practicum/Field work.
8. This includes teaching practice programme, working with community.
9. Social Service and work-experience. The Weightage for theory i.e. foundation course component is only 20%.
10. Forty per cent weightage has been given to Practicum/ Field work.
11. There is no scope for general education in the teacher education curriculum at the secondary level which is one-year course only.
12. Adequate attention to content enrichment is given in teacher education programme at the elementary level.
13. Curricula of teacher education either at the elementary/ secondary level is outdated.
14. Knowledge provided in these programmes is of very limited value in actual classroom settings.
15. The functional utility of the curriculum is limited and needs to improve by revising the curriculum, taking into consideration the task of teachers.
16. Curricular and co-curricular programmes need to be developed on certain sound principles.

MODEL ANSWERS

1. (i) (a) Advances in pedagogical science
   (b) Changes in objectives of school education
   (c) Improving functionality of teacher education programme
   (ii) Adult Education
   (iii) School Experience programme emphasises that prospective teachers need to be provided experiences not only in learning to teach, but also to perform other roles expected of them outside the classroom. Practice-teaching programme is narrow in scope. It aims at providing experiences to prospective teachers in learning to teach only.
2. (i) The need for general education at the elementary teacher education level is there because the minimum qualifications for admission to teacher education programme is 10+2. Further, elementary teachers are expected to teach upper primary classes also.
3. (i) Principle of relevance, principle of utility, principle of variety, principle of flexibility, etc.
   (ii) Debates, celebration of festivals, programmes of dramas, dance and music, games, visit to educational institutions.
   (iii) (a) to identify skills needed to organise co-curricular activities
   (b) to acquire the requisite skills
   (c) to understand the purpose for which co-curricular activities are organised in schools
   (d) to develop understanding that some pupils who may not be good in scholastic achievement, may have talent in certain fields like singing, dancing, etc.

KEYWORDS

General Education. Stands for content of different subjects taught in a school.

Prospective Teachers. The term prospective teachers stand for students of training college.

Elementary Teacher Education. Stands for teacher education programme which aims at preparing teachers to teach classes from I to VIII.

Practicum. The term stands for practical work and consists of field work.

Cognitive Development. Cognitive development refers to intellectual development.

NPE (1986). NPE stands for National Policy on Education (1986).

REFERENCES

Davis, James R. (1970). *Teaching Strategies for the Classroom*, Westview Press.

Jangira, N.K. and Singh, Ajit (1984). *Core Teaching Skills-Micro-Teaching Approach*, New Delhi (NCERT).

NCERT (1978). *Teacher Education Curriculum: A Framework*, New Delhi.

——— (1984). *Curriculum and Evaluation*, New Delhi.

——— (1987). Report of the Working Group on Revitalisation and Modernisation of Pre-service Teacher Education, New Delhi (Mimeo).

——— (1991). *Elementary Teacher Education Curriculum—Guidelines and Syllabi*, New Delhi.

———. *Secondary Teacher Education Curriculum—Guidelines and Syllabi*, New Delhi.

Singh, R.P. (1993). *The Challenges of Tomorrow: A Profile of Further Teacher Education*, New Delhi: Sterling Publisher Private Ltd.

Singh, L.C. (Ed.) (1990). *Teacher Education in India: A Resource Book*, NCERT, New Delhi.

FURTHER READINGS

Adaval, S.B. (1984). *Analytical Study of Teachers' Education in India*, Amitabh Prakashan, Allahabad.

Bhattacharya, G.C. (1990). *Teacher Education*, Vinod Pustak Mandir, Agra, U.P.

Burton, K. (1979). *Teaching-Learning Process* (in S.S. Chauhan: Innovations in Teaching-Learning Process. Vikash Publishing House Pvt. Ltd., New Delhi.

Davis, I.K. (1971). *The Management of Learning*, McGraw Hill Book Co., London.

Gage, N.L. (1963). *Paradigms for Research on Teaching,* Rand, MC Nally & Co., Chicago.

Good, C.V. (Ed. 1995). *Dictionary of Education*, McGraw Hill Book Co., New York.

Gupta, A.K. (1988). *Teacher Education*, Sterling Publishers, New Delhi.

Morrison, A. and McIntyre, D. (1969). *Teacher and Teaching*, Armond, Worth, Penguin.

Passi, B.K. (1976). *Becoming Her Teacher: Micro-teaching—Approach*, Sahitya Mudranalaya, Ahmedabad Gujarat.

Sharma, R.A. (2003). *Teacher Education*, International Publishers House, Meerut (U.P.).

Chapter 3

Development of Teacher Education

STRUCTURE OF CHAPTER

- Introduction
- The Secondary Education Commission (1952-53)
- National Council of Educational Research and Training
- Education and National Development (1964-66)
- National Policy on Education (1968)
- National Council for Teacher Education (1973)
- The Working Group to Review Teachers Training Programmes in the light of the Need for Value Orientation (1983)
- The Teacher and Society (National Commission on Teacher-I)
- Summary
- Evaluate Yourself
- Key Words
- References
- Further Readings

INTRODUCTION

Like other profession we need to know the history of development of teacher education institution. The first teacher training imitation was established by the Danish Mission under the leadership of Ziegenbalg in 1716 at Tranquebar. The Government started the first normal school in Madras in 1826. A normal school was started in Elphistone Institution 1847 at Bombay. Woods Despatch of 1854 suggested the establishment of teacher training system in India. By 1892, India had 116 training institutions for men and 15 for women. The Hunter Commission emphasised the training of teachers. Five teachers training colleges at Madras, Kurseong, Allahabad, Lahore, and Jabalpur were established according to the Government of India Resolution of Education Policy (1904). The Calcutta University Commission (1917), popularly known as Sadler Commission recommended the opening of department of education in universities. The department should have its own faculty of Professor and Reader. The demonstration school should be attached with the department for practical training and try-out of new methods of teaching.

The Commission recommended a postgraduate degree in education and introduction of education as optional subjects at B.A. Thirteen out of eighteen Universities started faculty of education on the recommendation of Sadler Commission. Bombay University started a postgraduate degree of M.Ed. in 1936. The Abbott-Wood Report 1937 made valuable suggestions about teacher training course, refresher course and community work. In 1941, the country had 612 normal schools and 25 training colleges. The Sargent Report of 1944 visualised a system of universal, compulsory and free education for all boys and girls of the age 6-14. It also suggested that suitable boys and girls should be given training for teaching after high school. The duration of training programme for pre-primary and junior basic school should be two years. The report suggested revised scales for teachers.

The University Education Commission of 1948 revised the position of secondary education. The course of teacher training was comprised of theory and practical. While there was no difference in theory, there was a lot of difference in practices followed in teacher training institution. The commission suggested that theory and practice should support each other.

Evaluate Yourself

(i) The first teacher training Institute was established in the year:

(a) 1617 (b) 1618 (c) 1716 (d) 1816

(ii) The education department should have its own faculty. This was recommended by:

(a) Wood Despatch

(b) Hunter Commission

(c) Resolution on Education Policy

(d) Sadler Commission

(iii) The University Education Commission was set up in the year:

(a) 1947 (b) 1948 (c) 1949 (d) 1950

THE SECONDARY EDUCATION COMMISSION (1952-53)

The Secondary Education Commission was appointed by the Government of India on 23rd September 1952 under the Chairmanship of Lakshmanswami Mudaliar. The member secretary of the Commission was A.N. Basu, Principal Central Institute of Education, Delhi. The terms of reference were:

(a) To enquire into and report on the present position of secondary education in all aspect, and

(b) Suggest measures for its reorganisation and improvement with particular reference to

- The aims, organisation and content of Secondary Education,
- Its relationship to Primary, Basic, and Higher Secondary,
- The inter relation of Secondary Schools of different types, and
- Other allied problems.

(c) So that a sound and reasonably uniform system of Secondary Education, suited to our needs and resources, may be provided for the whole country.

Based on these terms of reference, the Commission identified a few all-India problems in the light of article 45 of the Indian Constitution. The responsibility of the central government is greater in the field of teacher training. In the appraisal of the existing situation, the commission noted that nothing was done to train teachers for secondary schools during the years

1854-82. The Hunter Commission of 1882 and the University Commission of 1917 (Sadler Commission) did not solve the problem of training of teachers, their salaries, and coordination of services. The Hartog Committee of 1929 renewed the position of the training of teachers.

The report of Secondary Education Commission comprised of fifteen chapters. Two chapters "Improvement of Teaching Personnel" and "Dynamic Methods of Teaching" have been devoted to teachers and their training. The commission noticed the following three kinds of teacher training institutions in the country:

(i) Primary (for basic) Teacher Training Institutions

(ii) Secondary Teacher Training Institutions

(iii) Graduate Teacher Training Institutions

It was recommended that there should be only two types of teacher training institutions—(i) for those who have taken the School Leaving Certificate or Higher Secondary School Leaving Certificate, for whom the period of training should be two years, and (ii) for graduates, where the training may be of one academic year. Graduate teacher training institutes should be recognised by and affiliated to the universities which would grant the degree. The secondary grade training institution should be under the control of a separate board appointed for the purpose. (We may observe that the practice is prevailing even now).

The practical examination in teacher training institutions should comprise of practice in teaching; observation, demonstration and criticism of lesson; construction and administration of scholastic tests; organisation of supervisory study; conducting library period and maintenance of cumulative records. The student teacher should take special training in one or other of the co-curricular activities.

The teacher training institutions should accept the responsibility of organising:

(1) refresher courses,

(2) short intensive courses in special subjects,

(3) practical training workshop, and

(4) seminar and professional conferences; training institutions should be in close liaison with the department of education.

The training colleges should conduct research work in various aspects of pedagogy, and for this purpose it should have the experimental or demonstration school under its control. The staff of the colleges should be capable of devoting some of their time to research co-curricular and extracurricular activities, modern trend of pedagogy, and evaluate results of a particular method of training.

The postgraduate course in education leading to the degree of Master of Education (M.Ed.) is intended for higher studies in pedagogy. The course should:

- provide ideas to the study of comparative education of modern method;
- cultivate aptitude for research so that experiments on new methods and technique of education may be undertaken;
- specialise in one of the following branches:

  (a) curriculum, (b) craft-centred education,
  (c) co-curricular activities

The methods of teaching in schools should aim at imparting knowledge in an efficient manner. They should also aim at inculcating desirable values, proper attitude, and habit of working in the students. The teacher should be provided a training in these methods. Special part-time training courses should be organised to meet the shortage of teachers. The selection and appointment procedure should be uniform for all schools. The teacher possessing the qualification and performing the same type of work should be treated at par in the matter of grades of salary.

The recommendation of secondary education created a climate of equality and liberty in the matter of training of teachers. The education for character development was emphasised in subsequent years.

Evaluate Yourself

1. What should be the composition of practical programme in teacher training?
2. What type of programmes should be organised for in-service education of teachers?
3. What are the expectations of Secondary Education Commission from the holders of Masters Degree in Education?

NATIONAL COUNCIL OF EDUCATIONAL RESEARCH AND TRAINING (NCERT)

The National Council of Educational Research and Training (NCERT) was established in 1 September 1961 as an autonomous organisation. The council is fully funded by the Government of India.

The NCERT functions as an academic adviser to the Ministry of Human Resource Development, Government of India. In the formation and implementation of policies and programmes in the field of school education and teacher education, the Ministry counts upon on the expertise of the NCERT to a considerable extent.

According to annual report (1990-91)—The qualitative improvement of school education and teacher education is one of the major concerns of NCERT. As part of its efforts to bring about qualitative improvement in school education, the Council:

- conducts, aids and co-ordinates research in all branches of school education and teacher education;
- organizes pre-service and in-service training of teachers, mainly at the advanced level;
- organizes extension services for institutions, organizations and agencies engaged in educational reconstructions;
- develops and experiments with improved educational technique, practices and innovations;
- collects, compiles, processes and disseminates educational information;

- assists the State/UT governments and State/UT-level institutions, organizations and agencies in developing and implementing programmes for qualitative improvement of school education;
- collaborates with international organizations like UNESCO, UNICEF, UNDP, UNEPA and with national-level educational institutions of other countries;
- extends facilities for training and studies to educational personnel from other countries;
- serves as the academic secretariat of the National Council for Teacher Education (NCTE) and National Development Group (NDG) for the Asia and the Pacific Programme of Educational Innovations for Development (APEID), UNESCO, Bangkok.

The functions of the NCERT broadly relate to: (a) research and development, (b) in-service and pre-service training, and (c) extension and dissemination work—all these tuned to achieve the main objective of improving the quality of school education. The NCERT, therefore: (i) develops curriculum, instructional and exemplar materials, methods of teaching, techniques of evaluation, teaching aids, kits and equipments, learning resources, etc.; (ii) organises pre service and in-service training of teachers, teacher educators and other educational personnel; (iii) conducts and promotes educational research; (iv) disseminates improved educational techniques and practices and research findings; (v) acts as a clearing house for ideas and information on all matters relating to school education and teacher education. The constituent units of the council are:

(a) National Institute of Education (NIE), New Delhi
(b) Central Institute of Educational Technology (CIET), New Delhi
(c) Regional Institute of Education (RIE), Ajmer
(d) Regional Institute of Education (RIE), Bhopal
(e) Regional Institute of Education (RIE), Bhubaneshwar
(f) Regional Institute of Education (RIE), Mysore

According to the annual report of the council (1992), the National Institute of Education (NIE), New Delhi, had the following Department/Units involved in research, development, training, extension, evaluation, and dissemination activities in their specific areas of work:

1. Department of Education in Social Sciences and Humanities (DESSH)
2. Department of Education in Science and Mathematics (DESM)
3. Department of Pre-School and Elementary Education (DPSEE)
4. Department of Non-Formal Education and Education of the Scheduled Castes and the Scheduled Tribes (DNFEE SC/ST)
5. Department of Vocational of Education (DVE)
6. Department of Teacher Education, Special Education and Extension Services (DTESEES)
7. Department of Measurement, Evaluation, Survey and Data Processing (DMES & DP)
8. Department of Educational Psychology, Counselling and Guidance (DEPC & G)
9. Department of Women's Studies (DWS)
10. Department of Policy Research, Planning and Programming (DPRPP)
11. Planning, Programming, Monitoring and Evaluation Division (PPMED)
12. Department of Field Services and Extension Coordination (DFSEC)
13. Department of Library, Documentation and Information (DLDI)
14. Publication Department (PD)
15. Workshop Department (WD)
16. Navodaya Vidyalaya Cell (NVC)
17. Journal Cell (JC)
18. International Relations Unit (IRU)

The Central Institute of Educational Technology (CIET), headed by a Joint Director functions as one of the constituent units of the NCERT. The CIET has the following major divisions:

(i) Educational Television Division

(ii) Distance Education, Planning, Coordination, Research and Evaluation, Scripting and Training Division

(iii) Educational Radio Division

(iv) Graphics, Exhibition, Photo and Film Division

(v) Information and Documentation Division

(vi) Technical Planning, Operations and Maintenance Division

One of the major concerns of the council is the development of innovative programmes of pre-service teacher education. The Regional Institute of Education (RIEs) have been engaged in research studies related to the different aspects of schools education and teacher education; development of instructional materials for the use of teacher educators, teachers and teacher trainees; training and extension activities for qualitative improvement of school education and teacher education. Each Regional College of Education caters to the educational needs of the States/Union Territories under its jurisdiction. The RIE at Ajmer offers a 4-year integrated course in science education leading to the B.Sc. (Hons/Pass), B.Ed., Degree: a 1-year course leading to the B.Ed. degree with specialisation in Science/Agriculture/Commerce/Language (English/Hindi/Urdu), and a 1-year M.Ed. course with specialisation in Science/Commerce/Languages.

The RIE Bhopal offers pre-service programmes of a 4-year B.Ed. integrated course in Science and Arts, 1-year B.Ed. course in Science and Commerce, B.Ed. one-year course in Elementary Education, M.Ed. with specialisation in Science Education, Teacher Education, Guidance and Counselling and Elementary Education.

The RIE Bhubaneshwar offers pre-service programme of B.A. B.Ed. (4-year integrated course) Pass & Honours, B.Sc. B.Ed. (4-year integrated course) Pass & Honours, B.Ed. (course), B.Ed. (Elementary) Arts & Science (1-year B.Ed. course).

The RIE Mysore offers a 4-year integrated course in Science Education leading to the B.Sc. Ed. Degree; a 4-year integrated course in English Education leading to the B.A. Ed. degree; a 1-year B.Ed. course; a 1-year M.Ed. course; 2-year M.Sc. Ed. courses in Science Facilities for doing doctoral work are also available in all the four RIEs. All the RIEs conduct in-service training programmes both for school teachers and teacher educators. Each Regional Institute of Education has a demonstration multipurpose school attached to it. Teacher-trainees enrolled in various teacher education course, offered by three RIEs undergo practical training at the Demonstration Multipurpose Schools. These schools act as laboratories for trying out innovative practices in school education and teacher education.

Evaluate Yourself

1. What are the constituent units of the NCERT?
2. What are the broad areas of function of the NCERT?
3. What are the courses offered by Regional Institute of Education?

EDUCATION AND NATIONAL DEVELOPMENT (1964-66)

The report of Kothari Commission (1964-66) contains one complete chapter on teacher education. The recommendation about teacher education are related to improvement of quality of teacher education, removal of isolation of teacher education, improving the quality of training institutions, continuing professional education of teachers, and maintenance of standards in teacher education.

The commission was of the opinion that a sound professional programme of teacher education is essential for qualitative improvement of school education. The following major weaknesses were identified:

- Teacher Training Institutions remained isolated from main stream of the academic life of the university and the daily problem of the schools.
- The quality of teacher training institutions remained with a few exceptions, mediocre or poor.

- Competent staff were not attracted towards teacher institutions.
- Curriculum continued to be traditional and lacking vitality and realism.
- Rigid practice teaching was coupled with set practices.
- Training programme was not related with present day needs and objectives.

Removing the Isolation of Teacher Training

A comprehensive programme of teacher education was suggested to overcome the above deficiencies. The teacher education needs to be under the university system; the primary teacher education may be the concern of universities. The secondary education, though it is under university, but is separated from other disciplines. The university is providing step-motherly treatment to the education departments carrying out teacher training. The education is identified with pedagogy.

The intellectual academicians think that education is to be studied by those who have decided to enter into teaching professions. Education has developed as a social science and a separate academic discipline. Education is an instrument of change—social political and economic. Education is an intellectual discipline of scientific and philosophical importance. Education is to be introduced as an elective subject at graduate and postgraduate level.

Though many universities are now offering are master's degree in educations but full-fledged departments, or schools of education are yet not in operation as envisaged by the commission on the following lines:

- To conduct graduate and undergraduate course in education with a provision of minimum teaching practice as compulsory laboratory work.
- To organise courses in professional education for different categories of teachers—pre-primary, primary, and secondary.
- To provide extension services to institutions of teacher education.

- To organise summer institutes and in-service programmes in content areas and professional education.
- To work in close collaboration with schools to develop research-based curriculum and techniques of teaching.
- To promote inter-disciplinary research in education.

Eminent professors of different disciplines may be appointed as part time teachers in the schools of education to explain new developments in their field and to get these incorporated at school stages with appropriate modifications. This measure will improve professional education and break isolation of the university.

Each teacher training institute should establish an extension department. Each teacher training institution should be made responsible to guide the neighbourhood schools in planning their work and in using improved methods of teaching. The extension work is needed to improve the school as well as the teacher training programme. All members of the teacher training institution should participate in the extension programme.

Institutes of teacher education should have an effective alumni association. This will promote the constant touch and harmony with teacher education institutions. The old students may discuss problems of common interest with the faculty members. The sharing of experiences will benefit the faculty members to improve the training programme, otherwise found difficult in implementation. This will also provide an opportunity to follow up of the scheme planned and conducted during training period.

The programme of student teaching may be converted into comprehensive internship, the trainees should actively participate and observe the entire work of the school; the internship programme is only possible when the schools and teacher training colleges work in close collaboration and cooperation. They both should feel the responsibility of providing training to the students. The selected teachers of cooperating school may join the training college on deputation. The training college staff may conduct the research in the cooperating school.

There exists a total differentiation between primary and secondary teacher training institutions. The status of primary teacher training institution may be raised to a collegiate standard. All teacher education should come under the university and function in close collaboration with the state departments of education and teachers organisation. This will raise the standard and efficiency of the teacher education programmes.

Thus, to break the barriers of teacher education institutions from universities, schools and one another, the commission suggested following three measures:

(i) Comprehensive colleges of education should be established.

(ii) Pre-primary and primary teacher training institutions should be upgraded to collegiate standard.

(iii) State Board of teacher education may be established to:

- Prescribe standards for training institution
- Improve curriculum and programmes
- Prescribe condition for recognition
- Prepare plan for development of teacher education, both qualitative and quantitative.

Improving the Quality of Teacher Education

The poor quality of teachers is a source of overall deterioration in educational standards. Therefore, the programme of improvement of quality of teacher education should be given the highest priority and importance. Some broad principles are given below to recognise teacher education:

- Reorientation of subject knowledge in collaboration with university departments, leading to insight into basic concepts, objectives, and implications.
- Vitalization of professional studies, supported with research on problems under Indian conditions, and bridge the gap between theory and practice.
- Improvement of methods of teaching and evaluation.
- Improvement of student teaching programme to make it comprehensive internship programme with the stress on supervision.

- Development of special courses and programmes particularly on promotion/posting as headmaster, teacher educator, etc.
- Revision of curriculum at all levels of teacher education according to the objectives of preparing teachers for varied responsibilities.

Certain other measures are also required to improve the quality of teacher education. The number of working days need to be 230 in a teacher training institution. The duration of elementary teacher education and secondary teacher education programme may be two and one year respectively.

Improving the Quality of Training Institution

An urgent need is there to improve the quality of teacher training institutions, both secondary and primary. Early steps should be taken on the following lines:

(i) **Secondary Teacher Training Institutions:** The faculty of a secondary training college should possess double Masters degree in an academic subject and in education. A good number of them should have a doctorate. In order to develop supply line, scholarship should be made available to good students to attract them for M.Ed. and M.A. in Education. Qualified specialists may be appointed in these institutions by relaxing degree in education. Summer institutes should be arranged for the in-service education of the faculty. The best and most competent persons should be selected to teach in training institution.

(ii) **Primary Teachers Training Institutions:** The teachers trained for secondary stage generally provide training in Primary Training Institutes. They are inadequately prepared for primary stage. The staff of primary teachers training institution, should be adequately trained for their work of preparing primary teachers. The faculty of these institutions should be in the pay scales of college lecturers.

(iii) **General Recommendations:** Tuition fees should not be charged, and provision of scholarships and loans should be created in primary and secondary teacher training institutions. Experimental or demonstration schools should be attached with all teacher training colleges. Hostel facilities for students and residential accommodation for staff should be provided. Provision of libraries, laboratories and workshop should be improved.

In-service Education of School Teachers

Due to continuous evolution of pedagogical theory and practice and advances in all fields of knowledge, there is a strong need of in-service education of teachers. Therefore, every teacher should be able to receive at least two or three months in-service education in every five years of service. The curriculum of these in-service programmes should be planned and organised systematically. The instructional material should be developed with great care. The organizing faculty must be property oriented for the task to be completed and achieve it through in-service education of teachers. The teachers should be exposed to good textbook and audio-visual material.

Very little is being done for in-service education of primary teachers. This should receive top priority. Follow up of training programmes should be arranged. The organizers and resource persons must remain in touch with the teachers to exchange experiences. A news bulletin may be published to facilitate exchanges.

Research should be carried out on continuing in-service education of teachers and the result of research study should be made available to the teachers. The teachers should be encouraged for experimentation in their own schools.

Maintenance of Standards in Teacher Education

Organizations for maintenance of standards in teacher education are required at state and national level. The State Board of Teacher Education may be entrusted with the responsibility of raising of standards at State Level. The UGC, in collaboration with the NCERT, should set up a joint standing committee on teacher education. The Standing committee on

Teacher Education should have the following powers related with all aspects of teacher education:

1. To develop and establish standard for training institution and university departments.
2. To co-ordinate and improve standards of teacher education at all levels.
3. To advise universities and State Departments of Teacher Education regarding programmes, curricula, etc.
4. To grant funds to teachers' colleges, departments or schools of education in the universities.
5. To develop and support financially the programmes for the in-service department of teacher education and teachers.

The Government of India should provide funds in the centrally sponsored sector to assist state governments to develop teacher education.

State of Teachers

Continuous and intensive efforts are required to raise the economic, social and professional status of teachers. The remuneration of teachers should be enhanced. The pay scale of teachers working under different management should be uniform. Three main scales of pay were suggested: (a) Primary Teachers, (b) Trained Graduate Teachers, and (c) Postgraduate Teachers. The recruitment in schools with private management should be done by a duly constituted selection committee. The improved promotional prospects should be created for teachers in order to attract and retain men and talent. A qualified primary school teacher needs to be promoted as headmaster or inspector. A trained graduate teacher, who have done outstanding work, should be eligible for the salary of postgraduate teacher. The dearness allowance paid to the teachers should be at par with other government employees.

The system of retirement benefits to teachers should be uniform and at par with other government employees. The conditions of work in educational institutions should be such as to enable teachers to function at their highest level of efficiency. Professional organization of teachers which carryout work for the improvement of the profession and education should be recognised. The Ministry of Education should increase the number of national awards. Some of the recommendation of the Kothari Commission were implemented.

Many states came forward to set up State Boards of Teacher Education. Master's Degree Course in Education was introduced in many universities like Kurukshetra, Kanpur, etc. Many recommendations about status of teachers were implemented.

Evaluate Yourself

1. What are the major weaknesses in the teacher education programme according to Kothari Education Commission?
2. What are the steps recommended to remove the isolation of teacher training institutes by the Kothari Education Commission?
3. What are the major principles around which teacher education is to be reorganised?

NATIONAL POLICY ON EDUCATION (1968)

The Government of India issued a resolution on the Report of the Education Committee. The resolution is called the first National Policy on Education. The terms of reference of Education Commission was to advise the government on "The National Pattern of Education and on the general principles and policies for the development of education at all stages and in all aspects". The report 'Education & National Development' was discussed and commented upon. The general consensus emerged on the National Policy on Education.

The Policy contained seventeen principles. The following principles had implications for teacher education:

(i) Free and compulsory education
(ii) Equalization of educational opportunity
(iii) Production of books
(iv) Examination
(v) Secondary education
(vi) Spread literacy and adult education

(vii) The education structure

(viii) Status emoluments and education of teachers.

The quality of teachers determine the quality of education. A teacher is the most important factor to contribute to the material development. The success of all efforts to education depends upon the personal quality and character, educational qualifications and professional competence of a teacher. Teachers should be accorded an honourable place in the society.

The emoluments and service conditions of teachers should commensurate to the qualification and responsibilities. Not only this, but the emoluments and service conditions should also be adequate and satisfactory.

The teachers should be provided protection to speak and write about significant national and international issues. The teacher should be given academic freedom to pursue and publish independent studies and research.

Finally, the teacher education, particularly in-service education, should receive the due emphasis.

During the seventies, the implementation of National pattern of education i.e. 10+2+3, created a rethinking about the teacher education. Centres of continuing education were established in colleges of teacher education. These centres received funds from NCERT and state governments to organise in-service training programmes for the teachers.

Evaluate Yourself

1. The quality of teachers determine, the quality of.......

   (a) Student (b) Institution (c) Society (d) Education

2. The teachers should be protected to speak and write about National Issues.

   (a) Politics (b) Religion
   (c) National Issues (d) Responsible

NATIONAL COUNCIL FOR TEACHER EDUCATION (1973) (NCTE)

Government of India set up National Council for Teacher Education in 1973 with the education minister as president. The following were the terms of reference of the NCTE:

(i) To advise the Government of India on all matters concerning teacher education, including pre-service and in-service training, evaluation of curricula for teacher education and periodical review of progress in revising curricula.

(ii) To review the progress of plan schemes, both central and state, concerning teacher education.

(iii) To advise state government on any matter referred to the council by them.

(iv) To advise government on ensuring adequate standards in teacher education.

(v) Any other matter entrusted to the council by the Government of India.

The secretariat of the NCTE was located in the Department of Teacher Education, NCERT. The secretariat was expected to assist the NCTE by way of collecting data, preparing working papers and making surveys and field study to the work of the council. The council established the following six standing committees at the beginning:

(i) Standing Committee on standards in teacher education which should also act as the steering committee for the following.

(ii) Standing Committee on Elementary Teacher Education

(iii) Standing Committee on Secondary Education

(iv) Standing Committee on Pre-School Teacher Education.

(v) Standing Committee on Technical, Vocational & Work Experience

(vi) Standing Committee on In-service Education.

Subsequently, a Standing Committee for Training of teachers for Special School was also set up.

These standing committees worked for the improvement of teacher education in their respective areas. The NCTE made a significant contribution by modernising the curriculum of teacher education. The document Teacher Education Curriculum—A Framework (1978) contained the general and statewise objective of teacher education. Salient recommendations included in the document to improve the standard of teacher education are:

(i) Relevance of the curriculum to the personal and social need of children and schools.
(ii) Flexibility within the framework of acceptable national goals and values.
(iii) Interdisciplinary and integrated approach in teacher education.
(iv) Education as a discipline
(v) Semester system
(vi) Evaluation
(vii) Experiments, Innovations, and Research for development.

During the year 1988, NCTE brought out revised draft of National Curriculum for Teacher Education—a framework. The NCTE recommended that B.Ed. correspondence courses should be closed down with immediate effect. The 1st degree in teacher training cannot be provided through correspondence. The council developed a draft of code of professional ethics.

In the NPE (1986), it was recommended that NCTE should be made a statutory body. A bill to this effect was placed before the parliament in November 1992.

Evaluate Yourself

1. What were six standing committees of NCTE?
2. What is the opinion of NCTE about training of teacher through correspondence course?

THE WORKING GROUP TO REVIEW TEACHERS TRAINING PROGRAMMES IN THE LIGHT OF THE NEED FOR VALUE ORIENTATION

The Ministry of Education and Culture, Government of India, year 2014, constituted a group to review the teachers training programmes in light of the need for value orientation. The following were the terms of reference:

(i) To suggest the necessary changes to the present content and scope of value-orientation in education, with special reference to the need of ensuring development and promotion among students and teachers, not only of the highest values of physical, emotional, mental, aesthetic, moral and spiritual culture but also of those values which are uniquely Indian, and which would promote secularism, pride in heritage and composite culture.

(ii) To suggest a programme of the study of the national freedom struggle.

(iii) To suggest the curriculum content for teacher trainees to achieve the desired value orientation.

(iv) To suggest special technique of pedagogy for training in value-orientation.

(v) To suggest strategies for reorienting serving teachers through in-service programmes.

(vi) To suggest ways of promoting participation of voluntary organisations in organising training courses for teachers.

(vii) To assess dimensions of effort required and also to indicate the extent of governmental inputs.

(viii) To make suggestions which would be relevant to the determination of the new roles of teachers as counsellors and guides instead of being just lecturers.

(ix) To determine the important tasks that teachers will need to undertake towards preparing the new educational materials keeping in view the challenges of our times.

The NCERT was entrusted with the responsibility of providing facilities and materials for the proper functioning of the working group. The working group clarified the terms of reference and the basic ideas mentioned therein. It was stressed that value-oriented education is essential for effecting a radical change in the Indian society. The teachers' training programme should be modified to enable the teacher learn and transmit values essential for the progress of the country.

Certain basic ideas were clarified by the committee. The most important term was value. The word value is referred to as desirable ideals and goals which are intrinsic in themselves and which, when achieved or attempted to be achieved, evoke a deep sense of fulfilment to one or many or all parts of the highest elements of the nature. The entire realm of values—physical, emotional, intellectual, imaginative, aesthetic, moral, and spiritual were considered by the working group. The group suggested the transmission of values through subtitle and psychological means:

The working group spelled out a core programme of value-education. The programme of value orientation for teachers was divided into twelve components—values of relation to science, philosophy, psychology, morality, religion, spirituality, art, works of community service, courage and heroism, culture environment, and care of the material life. The pupil teachers and students should be brought nearer to the realisation of the ideals on all the occasions of daily life.

The role of teacher is more than of a skilled worker. The teacher should formulate short and striking words and ideas which should provide a stimulating atmosphere and present his own uplifting example. This group also envisaged a new system of evaluation comprising of written test, oral test, and project report. The group has suggested inclusion of Indian History as one of the subject in teachers training programme.

Some of the main recommendations made by the working group are as follows:

(i) The curriculum relating to value-education and to the study of Indian culture, should be immediately implemented in all the teachers training institutions.

(ii) Until the training institutions are remodelled on new lines as suggested in the report, an interim measure is recommended, under which the teacher training institutions should offer three new papers related to: philosophy and psychology of value-oriented education, Indian values as optional papers in place of any other three papers which are at present prescribed in the teachers training programme.

(iii) Two streams of teachers training programme should be initiated: (a) 4 years teacher education programme after senior secondary, (b) 2 years teacher education programme after graduation.

(iv) Pioneering and pace setting value-oriented institutions should be established, preferably one in each state.

(v) A few national institutes of teacher education should be designed and established, especially to educate the staff of the colleges of teacher education in India.

(vi) An All-India Public Examination for the evaluation of teacher trainees should be instituted.

(vii) Measures should be taken to eliminate various evils and deficiencies which are growing alarmingly in teachers training institutions.

(viii) It is further recommended that the present National Council of Teacher Education may itself be reconstituted.

The working group also suggested the creation of National Organisation for Teachers Training with the following objectives:

(a) To keep under review the institutions and programmes of teacher education in the country at all levels and to maintain high standards of teaching, research and examinations in the field of teacher education.

(b) To establish and to maintain: (i) Institutes of Teacher Education designed especially to educate the staff of the colleges of teacher education in India; (ii) pace-setting model institutions of teacher education.

(c) To provide aid—financial, material, and human; necessary advise for coordination and maintenance of high standards of teaching, examination, and research; to stimulate thinking on problems of teacher education.

(d) To function as an accrediting authority with powers to recognise teacher training institutions and degree awarded by them.

(e) To conceive of and implement programmes of strategies for bringing the existing teacher education institutions to conform to the aims and objective laid down by the council.

(f) To perform such other functions as may be conducive to the realisation of the aims and objectives of teacher education.

The working group recommended that the government should take urgent steps for the implementation of the recommendations. The recommendation of the working group had serious implications. The educationist thought seriously for value-oriented teacher education.

Evaluate Yourself

1. What are the core components of value education programme?
2. What are the three papers suggested by the group for value oriented teacher education course?
3. What are the two streams of teacher training programme?

THE TEACHER AND SOCIETY (NATIONAL COMMISSION ON TEACHERS I)

The Government of India set up two National Commissions on Teachers in 1983. National Commission on Teachers I (1983-85) under the Chairmanship of D.P. Chattopadhyaya submitted its report titled "The Teacher and Society." The Commission elaborated national goals and role of the teacher. The teachers should be prepared for national goals of a united secular India, a modern nation, and a humane and caring society.

The commission laid down criterion for the selection of candidates for training of teachers as good physique, linguistic and communication skills, a fair degree of general mental ability, general awareness of the word, a positive outlook on life and capacity of good human relations. The trainees should be selected on the basis of a test followed by group discussion and interview. The duration of the 1-year B.Ed. course needs to be extended by two summer months ensuring an academic session of 220 days with longer working hours. The teacher training programme of 4-year integrated course should be promoted by providing grants to enlarge and improve physical facilities. The integrated 4-year curriculum for a degree in education should contain the programme of general education and professional preparation.

The general education should include study of language, three or four disciplines from among the subjects taught at school, seminar, project and study visit. The professional education part should consist of study of education including educational psychology, sociology of education and philosophy of education, practice of teaching and its content-cum-methodology and learning a variety of skills related to the role of a teacher including educational technology and preparation of software.

The word practice teaching should be replaced by the word internship in teaching—a more comprehensive concept of teacher training. The duration of internship should not be less than four weeks in the third year and three weeks in the fourth year of study. The trainees should participate obligatorily in co-curricular activities. The performance of trainees should be evaluated in cognitive and affective areas.

The commission suggested the entry qualification for the admission to different courses of teacher education. The preparation of a teacher should be the joint responsibility of college of education and practice teaching school. The school teachers should be involved in the internship programme. They, in collaboration with teacher educators, should demonstrate teaching in the classroom on topics of choice. Thus, along with demonstration lesson, they need to share their rich experience with the trainees. The state department of education must support the colleges of teacher education in identifying practice teaching schools.

The principals and teachers of practice teaching schools need to be invited in the college of education to discuss the entire practice teaching programme and details should be worked out. The help of school should be sought in maintaining the record of trainees.

The commission discussed the qualification of teacher educators; various anomalies in the qualifications of teacher educator were sorted out. The college of education must have adequate number of qualified teacher educators according to the need for trainees. Adequate funds should be made available for this purpose. The teacher educators should be proficient in the use of skills they seek to develop among their trainees. They should also be proficient in the development of educational technology.

The curriculum for elementary teacher education should consist of general education and professional preparation. The trainees should acquire mastery over language and communication skills. The elementary schools are places of joy, play and activity. The trainees should learn to promote listening, observing and discovery. The teacher educators for the elementary training institutes should be drawn from practising primary schools.

The correspondence-cum-contact programmes could be organised for theoretical course with emphasis on practical aspect of training. This requires a reasonable infrastructure and meticulous planning of practice teaching with network of schools. The teacher educators for the task should be carefully selected for supervision and guidance. The organisers of correspondence-cum-contact programme may be used for promoting a variety of in-service programmes and in updating knowledge of teachers and teacher educators.

The following are the shortcomings of the existing M.Ed. (Master of Education) programme:

- The course does not have the rigour that a Master's degree ought to have.
- The course is not designed to meet clear professional ends.
- The course does not develop insight into the Indian educational scene.
- The course does not provide global understanding of crucial educational issues.

- The course does not process vocational attraction.
- The standard of teaching in this course is unsatisfactory.

There is a strong need to revamp the course of Master of Education. The course should be considered as an extension of the period of professional preparation. The course should also develop a high degree of specialization. The course should be geared to prepared experts like: (i) Teacher Educators, (ii) Curriculum consultants, (iii) Supervisors, (iv) Administrators.

The norms developed by the NCTE for the physical and staff resources are to be reviewed. These norms should be strictly followed and implemented.

The case for in-service education of teachers was discussed in detail. The facilities were inadequate quantitatively and poor from the point of relevance and effectiveness. The Centre of Continuing Education (CCE) carried out the job of training programme for primary teacher educators and for primary and secondary school teachers. The centres were closed subsequently. Recommendations were made about choices of resources, persons, training methodology, use of educational technology, and evaluation and follow up.

Composite pay scales for all categories of teachers and educational administrators were suggested to attract persons of ability and character to the profession. This recommendation enhanced the aspiration of the teachers.

The facility of study leave and teacher fellowship need to be extended for teachers to improve their knowledge and skills. Additional increment should be given to teachers who acquire higher qualification relevant to their work. Facility of family welfare measures in the form of scholarship towards job to dependent, etc. needs to be extended. Social security measures like housing and health care, may be provided. The status, working conditions and welfare benefits should be enhanced by necessary measures.

The performance of teacher will improve if he is aware of what the society expects of him. Teachers need to have a job security and academic freedom to perform their professional duties. Teachers should follow a code of conduct. A code of conduct should be developed in consultation with teachers organisation and needs to be strengthened with reference to in-service education, research and publication.

The recommendations of teacher commission about national goals, teachers' role, training of teachers, in-service education of teachers and society's expectations of the teachers are significant.

Evaluate Yourself

1. What are the criterion for the selection of candidate for a teacher training institution?
2. What should be the theoretical orientation of teachers?
3. Suggest measures for success of internship in teaching.

SUMMARY

1. At the initial stage of the development, the need for teachers training was emphasized by various commissions and committees.
2. The recommendations were made about creation of training facilities, establishment of department of teacher education, duration of teacher training and practice teaching.
3. The secondary education commission recommended an overall improvement of teachers and their training.
4. The Kothari Commission suggested steps for qualitative improvement of teacher education.
5. The recommendations created an awareness about improvement of status of teachers.
6. The establishment of the National Council Educational Research and Training by the Government of India is a milestone in the development of pre-service and in-service teacher education.
7. The Regional Colleges of Education started 4-year integrated courses for preparation of teachers.
8. National Policy on education 1986 was based on the report of the Kothari Commission.

9. The policy paved way for National System of Education. National Council for Teacher Education was created to ensure standards in teacher education and advise both the central and state governments on teacher education.
10. The working group to review teachers training programme stressed the need for value orientations, National Commission on Teachers–I equated all teachers and administrators by recommending a single pay scale.
11. Finally all commissions and committees set up upto 1985 recommended the improvement of facilities for pre-service and in-service teacher education.

MODEL ANSWERS

1. (i) c (ii) c (iii) b
2. (i) The practical programme in teacher training should include:
    - (a) practice teaching
    - (b) observation of lessons by the trainees
    - (c) demonstration lessons by the trainees
    - (d) criticism lesson
    - (e) construction and administration and analysis of scholastic tests in subjects
    - (f) organisation of supervised study for students
    - (g) conducting library period
    - (h) maintenance of cumulative record cards of students

   (ii) Programmes for in-service education of teacher:
    - (a) Refresher course
    - (b) Short intensive course in special subject
    - (c) Practical training workshop
    - (d) Seminar
    - (e) Professional conferences

   (iii) The holders of Masters degree in Education should be specialist in:

(a) Comparative education and modern method
(b) Research methodology
(c) One area of specialization from the following:
(i) curriculum (ii) craft centred education (iii) co-curricular activities.

3. (i) (a) National Institute of Education (NIE)
(b) Central Institute of Educational Technology (CIET)
(c) Regional Institute of Education (RIE)

(ii) Broad areas of functioning of the NCERT in school education and teacher education are:
(a) Research and development
(b) In-service and Pre-service training
(c) Extension

(iii) Regional Colleges of education offer
(a) 4-year integrated courses in teacher education leading to B.A./B.Sc. B.Ed. Degree
(b) 1-year course in teacher education leading to B.Ed. degree
(c) B.Ed. (Elementary) one-year course in Elementary Education
(d) M.Sc. Ed. (in selected subjects)

KEYWORDS

Normal School: Elementary Teacher Training Institute.

National Institute of Education (NIE): NIE is located at New Delhi in the campus of National Council of Educational Research and Training Sri Aurobindo Marg, New Delhi.

Regional Institute of Education: College of education established by the NCERT as its constituent unit which offers pre-service and in-service teacher education on the regional basis.

Four Year Integrated Courses: Courses offered after +2 for the preparation of teachers leading to a composite degree in the subject and education e.g. B.A. B.Ed. or B.Sc. B.Ed.

FURTHER READINGS

Barr, A.S. (1985). *Characteristics of Successful Teachers*, Phi Delta Kappan, March.

Bhattacharya, G.S. (1990). *Teacher Education*; Vinod Pustak Mandir, Agra (U.P.).

Gupta, A.K. (1988). *Teacher Education*, Sterling Publishers, New Delhi.

Kulshrestha, S.P. (1979). *Mini-teaching: A New Experiment in Teacher Education*, Research Monograph, Dehradun.

Ryan, D.G. (1969). *Characteristics of Teacher: A Research Study*, Sterling Publishing House Ltd. Delhi.

Saxena, N.R., Mishra, B.K. and Mohanty, R.K. (1988). *Teacher Education*, R. Lall Book Depot, Meerut.

Sharma, R.A. (1986). *Teacher Education*, International Publishing House, Meerut.

Shukla, R.S. (1978). *Emerging Trends in Teacher Education*, Chug Publication, Allahabad.

Skinner, B.F. (1968). *Technology of Teaching*, Appleton-Century-Crofts, New York.

Srivastava, S.S. (1988). *Shiksha Mein Nawachar Evam Adhunik Parivartan* (in Hindi), Har Prasad Bhargava, Agra.

Tibble, J.W. (1971). *Future of Teacher Education*, Routledge and Kegan Paul, London.

REFERENCES

Basu, A.N. (Ed.) (1952). Indian Education in Parliamentary Papers. Part 1. Bombay: Asia Publishing House.

Ministry of Education (1962). The Report of University Education Commission (1948-49). New Delhi: Govt. of India.

——— (1965). The Report of the Secondary Education Commission (1952-53). New Delhi: Govt. of India.

——— (1966). The Report of the Education Commission (1964-66), Education and National Development. New Delhi: Govt. of India.

——— (1967). The Report of the Committee of Members of Parliament of Education: National Policy on Education. New Delhi. Govt. of India.

Ministry of Education and Culture (1983). The Report of the Working Group to Review Teachers Training Programme (in the light of the Need for Value-Orientation). New Delhi: Govt. of India.

Mukherji, S.N. (1968). *Education of Teachers in India*, New Delhi: S. Chand & Co.

Nurullah, S. and Naik, J.P. (1951). *A History of Education in India*. New Delhi: Mac. Millan and Co.

NCERT (1984). National Council of Educational Research and Training, Memorandum of Association and Rules. New Delhi.

——— (1978). Teacher education Curriculum—A Framework Prepared for National Council for Teacher Education. New Delhi.

——— (1992). Annual Report of National Council of Educational Research and Training, (1990). New Delhi.

Singh, L.C. (Ed.) (1990). *Teacher Education in India—A Source Book*, New Delhi, NCERT.

Chapter 4

Evaluation of Teacher Education Programmes

STRUCTURE OF CHAPTER

- Introduction
- Measurement of Evaluation
- Types of Evaluation
- Purpose of Programme Evaluation
- Objectives and Criteria of Evaluation of Teacher Education Programme
- Techniques of Evaluation of the Teacher Education Programme
- Summary
- Model Answers
- Keywords
- References
- Further Readings

The National Policy on Education 1986 indicated an overhauling of teacher education. The first step in this direction is the replacement of existing teacher education institutions by new institutions namely, the district Institute of Education and Training, Colleges of Teacher education and Institute of advanced Study in Education. Steps for establishment and strengthening of departments of education in universities have already been initiated. The demand of the hour is qualitative improvement of teacher education programme.

INTRODUCTION

In order to understand the effectiveness of teacher education programme, we need to understand the effective teacher first. Combs (1965) defined the effective teacher formally as a unique human being who has learned to use himself effectively and efficiently to carry out his own society's purpose in the education of others. One interpretation of this definition is that the teacher needs to acquire competency and knowledge. The other definition is that he has to develop himself as a person and a professional. To educate a teacher, the teacher educator must help to develop self and learn to understand others. Successful attempts are made to identify competencies to train teachers. The acquisition and mastery over these competencies may lead to act effectively in the classroom. Accordingly teacher training programmes were devised. The competency-oriented teacher education was designed to hold teachers accountable to the process of education of children.

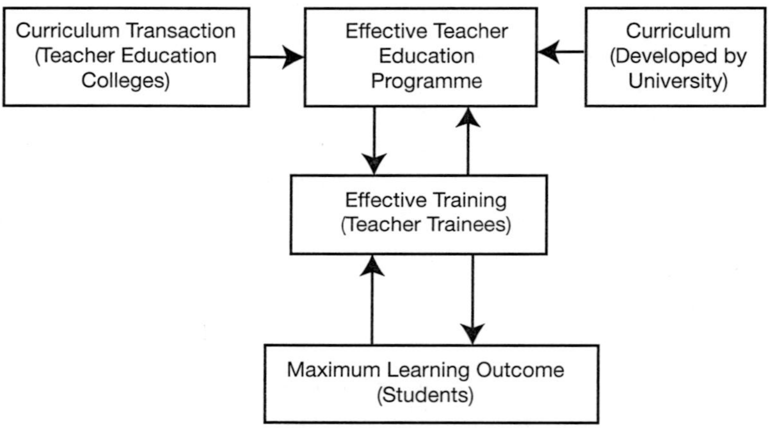

Fig. 4.1: Schematic Representation of Effective Teacher Education Programme.

Effective teaching means teaching which produces maximum learning outcomes. It aims to achieve the goals of education. Teacher's effectiveness means "ability to teach effectively in classroom." An effective teacher may be understood as one who helps development of the basic skills, understanding, proper work habits, desirable attitudes, and value judgement. Teacher effectiveness concerns with these outcomes and the objectives of education. It points to the effects of a teacher in a classroom situation.

The act of teaching and responses of students may be analysed into specific behaviour components. The behaviour components are developed through training in a teacher education institution. A systematic programme of teacher education is designed to develop essential skills and attitudes of teaching. Thus, an effective teacher education programme may prepare effective classroom teachers, who perform effectively in the classroom.

Evaluate Yourself

1. Who is an effective teacher?
2. What is effective teaching?
3. What are the components of the effective teacher education programme?

MEASUREMENT AND EVALUATION

Evaluation plays an important role in determining the progress of students, effectiveness of teaching and success of a programme. It influences teaching, learning process, curriculum development and research. In this sense, evaluation becomes a process directed towards the achievements of objectives. Thus, evaluation is a systematic process used for determining the success of objectives.

The evaluation may be both qualitative and quantitative. It is an estimation of progress of subjects towards objectives. The purposes of evaluation are:

(i) to collect evidence to show the degree of progress towards curricular goals.

(ii) to enable teacher educators to know about the effectiveness of teaching, experiences, activities, instructional methods and materials.

The concept of evaluation is different from the concept of examination, testing or measurement.

Measurement is a quantitative estimation of change in behaviour. The measurement is a process of assigning units. It is quantifying characters, attributes or dimensions in terms of units. The measurement is goal oriented and precise in terms of pre-determined units. Godde defined measurement as the comparison of a quantity with an appropriate scale for the purpose of determining the numerical value on the scale. Measurement is carried out by an instrument or tool. The tools may be called as observation schedule, rating scale, interview, achievement tests, inventory, checklist, etc. Thus, tools provide us measurement, which helps in evaluation.

Evaluation goes beyond measurement. Whereas measurement provides data base for evaluation, evaluation is purposeful, goals oriented and involves value judgement.

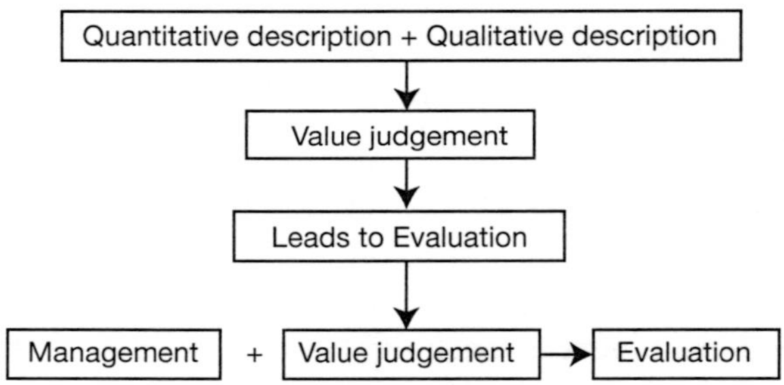

Fig. 4.2: Relationship between Measurement and Education.

Sometimes a teacher educator speaks from his experience without measurements of any characteristic, dimension or attribute about value judgement. This may lead to evaluation. But this evaluation may not be objective, reliable and valid. In that case, measurement becomes essential for evaluation.

Evaluation is value judgement and is based on objectives, which in turn determine the direction in which a programme, pupils or trainees should develop. The teachers guide their students in this direction. Then one can say that the objectives have been achieved. In developing a curriculum, objectives are defined first. The objectives become goals to be achieved and are concerned with the all-round development—social and physical. Objectives vary in range and quality from institution to institution. In order to come to an agreement, the objectives of evaluation may be concerned with knowledge, skills, interests and attitudes. Thus, objectives become guidelines in the areas of curriculum.

The curriculum analysis method is used to evaluate a curriculum. The purpose of curriculum is analysed into independent objectives. These objectives then are further converted into behaviour terms. The basic skills finally become the basis of evaluation.

Evaluation is a comprehensive process. It covers both scholastic and non-scholastic dimensions of pupils' or trainees' growth. The major objectives for evaluation are contents from the areas of concepts, knowledge and skills. This list of objectives is incomplete without the objectives belonging to the areas of appreciation, attitudes, interests and emotional—social adjustment. The requirement is of the development of subjects in all the dimensions. Techniques of evaluation are valid and reliable in the areas of knowledge, concept, skills and attitudes. Thus, it is very difficult to measure the entire educative experiences provided to the subjects in the institution. It will require lots of time and energy.

The teacher educators in a college of education can measure a sample of total behaviour. The sample should be comprehensive enough to help in accurate judgement according to the objectives of curriculum. The items of a test should be representative. The sum total items of concepts, knowledge and skills cannot be included in the test for want of time, energy and resources.

Fairly satisfactory tests for the measurement of concept, knowledge, skill and attitude are available now. Similarly tests for fairly reliable measurement of growth and development of trainees will also help in the refinement of techniques and tools of evaluation. The technique of sampling from the course has also improved. Thus, techniques, sampling and measurement are used to make evaluation comprehensive.

Growth and development are continuous processes. Hence, judgement about growth and development of trainees should also be continuous. This provides us a direction about evaluation, and it becomes an on-going process. The teacher educator now evaluates the progress of their trainees on day-to-day basis. The continuity of evaluation helps in modifying the activities prescribed in the curriculum which are not conducive to development. The collected evidence on the basis of measurement also affects the curriculum by indicating the areas in which trainees' achievement is not upon the mark as desired; the evaluation helps in modifying curriculum and redefining objectives.

The approach to evaluation is not rigid or static in nature; it should be flexible and dynamic. The type of examination, frequency of examination, tools for measurement and criterion for sampling of content, all should be dynamic. The behaviour of trainees in every learning situation is the concern of teacher educator. The acquisition of attitude interest and emotional stability is being affected by learning of content from different subject areas. The quality of behaviour is the concern of teacher educator and hence the procedure of evaluation should be flexible.

Evaluation should be cooperative. In any case, the effort to evaluate trainees in different dimensions of development is to be given importance. Tests are to be constructed for measurement, which requires the knowledge of different dimensions of development. The teachers educators may cooperate in the development of test battery. Similarly, several teacher educators have to cooperate in the construction of scales and determining criteria to measure the effectiveness of a curriculum programme.

Evaluate Yourself

1. What are the purposes of educational evaluation?
2. What is measurement?
3. What are the characteristics of educational evaluation?

TYPES OF EVALUATION

Three types of evaluation are used in an educational system.

(a) Preparative Evaluation
(b) Formative Evaluation
(c) Summative Evaluation

The purpose of preparative evaluation is to know the input required for the effective functioning of a programme. In a programme of teacher education, we require trainees, curriculum, and teacher education institution. In the teacher education institution, we need teacher educators and physical facilities. The qualification, experience and expertise of teacher educators play an important role in the curriculum transaction besides physical facilities.

The preparative evaluation is related to the competence of pupil teachers with reference to the requirement of a course. The entering behaviour is also determined by preparative evaluation. In colleges of education, an entrance test is conducted to determine the suitability of a candidate.

This may be termed as preparative evaluation. The practice of written test, group discussion and interview, which is followed in a few universities for admission to a course may be called as preparative evaluation, as it takes into account the qualification, aptitude and necessary skills required. Naturally, it is clear that this type of evaluation, is done for admission to a particular type of course at the commencement of a teaching learning programme.

The formative evaluation is done by teacher educators during the teaching learning process or formation of learning. Naturally, this type of evaluation provides feedback to the student teachers and teacher educators about learning. It helps in identifying the strength and weakness which results in modification of teaching and learning process. The frequent use of formative evaluation is very effective in determining the pace of learning for each student teacher. The trainees feel motivated and may try to achieve mastery over a unit of content.

The teacher educators modify their process of instruction on the basis of feedback given by formative evaluation. The periodical tests, assignment and tasks given in the teacher education colleges serve the purpose of formative evaluation. The practice teaching programme, where each and every lesson is supervised by the teacher educator and feedback is provided to the trainees, is a part of formative evaluation. The student teacher is encouraged to follow strong points and is suggested to modify week points in their classroom teaching.

This form of evaluation helps student teachers to improve their classroom behaviour. In this process, the teacher educator also gets the complete impression of classroom teaching of a student teacher and the effectiveness of his suggestions. The formative evaluation is most effective during the training programme as it motivates the trainees to put forth the necessary extra efforts at the appropriate time.

The annual examination conducted by a university, board or school at the end of a year or course may be called a summative evaluation. Summative evaluation is done at the end of a course or educational programme. The summative evaluation determines the success of a trainee or student in the course. Naturally, it takes place at the completion of a programme. This type of evaluation provides feedback for modification of objectives of teaching, learning process, or tools of evaluation.

The purpose of summative evaluation is certification or grading. In the colleges of education, the annual examination of theory papers conducted by the universities results in summative evaluation. The annual examination in practice teaching and work experience is also a part of summative examination. You may observe that some of the objectives listed in this chapter are not evaluated in the summative evaluation in the university examination patterns.

Evaluate Yourself

1. What is preparative evaluation?
2. What is formative evaluation?
3. What is summative evaluation?

PURPOSE OF PROGRAMME EVALUATION

The purpose of evaluating the effectiveness of a programme is to be determined in advance. The following three purposes may serve as guidelines:

(1) Improvement of the programme

(2) Maintenance of the programme

(3) Termination of the programme

Improvement of the programme based on evaluation. The maintenance of the programme indicates that the programme should continue as it serves the objectives for which it was planned. The third purpose is to terminate the programme after evaluation as it does not fulfil the objectives. In this process, the evaluators determine the standards of programme. In other words, they agree on the standard of the programme. They also notice a discrepancy in existence between programme and the expected standard. The process of evaluation is used to identify the weakness of the programme. Obviously, the planners of the teacher education programme or teacher educators have to ask continuously and frequently whether the programme keeps pace with the changing world in terms of competencies and interests required for the effective performance of the teacher's job.

Programme evaluation helps in making educational decisions and vice versa. These decisions may be related with change or modification of curriculum at a stage, change in plans and practices for future education, grade placement and promotion of subjects, change in self concepts of trainees about their abilities or effectiveness of an educational programme. On the basis of measurement and evaluation the following types of decisions are generally taken (Nunnally, 1964):

- Administrative Decisions
- Counselling Decisions
- Research Decisions
- Classroom Decisions

The administrative decisions are related with grade placement, continuity of a programme, addition or deletion of content or units. The teacher also takes decision about remedial work to be done by a student. A slow learner may be given extra time to master a content. In our country, minimum levels of learning have been decided and these are going to be used in the classroom intensively and extensively at elementary level. The teacher-made test plays an important role in taking decision about achievement of students. The teacher education colleges have to equip trainees for this type of measurement and decisions.

After independence, a movement for guidance and counselling has been generated. It is in slow speed but many students have started seeking counselling. The parents and teachers also support the movement. Tests of personality, interest and aptitude required for this purpose are generally standardized and are constructed by experts of the area. The inventories of personal problem are also designed by the specialists. These tests help students and counsellors in counselling and guidance work.

The researchers which may include teachers or teacher educators, conduct experiments to determine the effectiveness of different strategies of instructions. The psychologists do systematic studies in various approaches to education. They also want to make decisions about effectiveness, impact, development and attitude related to different aspects of education. Many types of standardized tests are required for the research.

The classroom decisions are based on teacher-made tests. The achievement tests are generally conducted by the teachers in different subjects and units. The result of these tests support the teachers.

The knowledge about nature and types of educational decisions helps the teacher educators and curriculum planners to evaluate effectiveness of a programme.

Evaluate Yourself

1. What are three purposes of programme evaluation?
2. What are the educational decisions influenced by programme evaluation?
3. What are the types of educational decisions?

OBJECTIVES AND CRITERIA OF EVALUATION OF TEACHER EDUCATION PROGRAMME

The objectives of teacher education programme determine the type of teachers being produced by a college of education or university. The objectives are framed on the basis of requirements felt by a university to serve the society and its schools. The expectations of the society from the teachers, their attitude towards teaching skills essential to carry out the responsibilities and value orientation, all are taken into consideration before planning a programme of teacher education.

The teaching learning process carried out in a teacher training institution involves three steps: (i) outcome of learning in terms of stated objectives (ii) planning of learning experiences to help trainees to attain stated objectives (iii) degree of achievement of learning experiences in terms of stated objectives. Naturally, the objectives have direct bearings on teaching, learning and evaluation. Learning experiences are organised and the outcome of learning is evaluated on the basis of objectives. Objectives determine planning of learning experiences and available physical facilities.

The B.Ed. programme of universities was planned with the following objectives according to Ordinances, Syllabus and Course of Reading, 2010: (The sequence of objectives have been changed and some of the objectives are slightly modified to understand them).

- To develop awareness among student teachers about the role of education in building up a democratic, secular, and socialistic pattern of society.
- (The student teacher needs) To acquire desirable social attitude and become an effective instrument of social change and develop understanding of his role in the modernising of Indian society.
- To develop understanding of psychological principles of growth and development, learning and transfer of training.
- To develop necessary skills, understanding, interests and attitudes enabling the pupil teacher (or student teacher) to foster all-round development of children under his care.
- (The student teacher needs) To acquire knowledge of Indian education system and the way it functions.
- (The student teacher needs) To possess sufficient competency and skills to guide pupils under his care in health, educational, recreational activities and work experience.
- (The student teacher needs) To develop skills and competencies to educational guidance and counselling.
- (The student teacher needs) To develop competency to teach effectively in accordance with the accepted

principles of teaching learning and using modern technology in teaching.

- (The student teachers needs) To develop skills in identifying, selecting, innovating and organising learning experience for teaching.
- (Finally, the student teacher needs) To acquire professional behaviour and to develop commitment to teaching profession.

The universities aim at preparing effective secondary school teachers, who are capable of responding to the changing needs of the modern Indian society. The B.Ed. programme has the following components:

- Pedagogical Theory
- Practice Teaching
- Practical work: (a) Black Board Writing, (b) Psychology practical
- Work experience

The course on pedagogical theory has four papers. The third paper has two portions: (A) compulsory (B) optional. The course offers eight options under paper III B. Selected objectives and topics of each paper are given below to understand the structure of the programme.

Paper I: Education in the Emerging Indian Society

Objectives

Objectives of this paper are under following:

(i) Discriminate among the various terms commonly used in education and to describe aims of education and their relevance in the context of present-day society.

(ii) Critically describe education as an agent of social change and to establish relationship between school and community programme.

(iii) Understand the process of national development, planning and the role of education.

In order to achieve these objectives, the content prescribed includes education and its aims in modern context, present day

Indian Society, planning, and national development. The various terms commonly used in education like training, instruction, schooling and indoctrination are contained in unit one. Education, as an instrument of social change, is also included as a topic under unit three.

Paper II: Educational Psychology

Objectives: Objectives of this paper are under below:

(i) Understand the process of learner's growth and development of Indian adolescents.

(ii) Explain and apply the concept of learning, various theories, laws and methods of learning.

(iii) Explain (and use) the concept of motivation, technology and devices of motivating the learner.

The content prescribed to achieve the above objectives includes psychology of development, psychology of learning, and psychology of motivation. The unit on psychology of development emphasises on learner's growth—intellectual, social and emotional, and development with special reference to Indian adolescents.

The paper has two components—theory and practical. The practical work is to be evaluated with other practical works externally.

Paper III A: Indian Education System—Structure and Problems

Objectives: Objectives of this paper are under below:

(i) To acquaint student teachers with the structure of Indian education—primary and secondary.

(ii) To acquaint student teachers with some contemporary issues.

(iii) To acquaint student teachers with major recommendations of various commissions and committees at school level.

In order to achieve the above objectives, units on primary education, secondary education, teacher education and some contemporary issues are included. Major recommendations of various commissions and committees are to be studied with reference to the above levels of education.

Paper IV: Essentials of Teaching Learning

Objectives: Objectives of this paper are under below:

(i) To acquaint student teachers with the concept of teaching and its ingredients.

(ii) To help student teachers to acquire various teaching skills.

(iii) To make student teachers conversant with educational technology and its classroom implications.

Paper V and VI: Content-cum-Methodology of Teaching Subject

Objectives: Objectives of this paper are under below:

(i) To enable the student teachers to formulate aims and objectives of teaching subject.

(ii) To enable the student teachers to understand and apply different methods of teaching.

(iii) To enable the student teachers to prepare different teaching aids and use them appropriately.

(iv) To enable the student teachers to prepare a good evaluation tool on a given topic.

The content-cum-methodology courses comprise of four units. These are as follows:

(i) Objectives of teaching

(ii) Methods and technique of teaching

(iii) Teaching aids

(iv) Evaluation

The list given above is not complete and only few objectives have been mentioned for illustrations. The objectives may be overlapping, but these objectives framed for each paper must contribute to the achievement of overall objectives of teacher preparation programme. Any objective may be further transformed into behavioural learning outcome to observe it. The observable behaviour is the achievement of any training programme.

Evaluate Yourself

1. What are the three steps involved in teaching learning process?
2. List five main objectives of the B.Ed. course.
3. What are the criteria of planning a teacher training programme?

TECHNIQUES OF EVALUATION OF THE TEACHER EDUCATION PROGRAMME

The most important contribution of evaluation during the recent years is the improvement of programmes. The systematic evaluation helps in the improvement. The application of systematic procedure provides basis for the development of a programme. Formative evaluation is most suitable for developmental programme as it helps in taking decisions about principles and practices of education.

The effectiveness of the total teacher education programme may be judged in terms of achievement of desired outcomes of total programme. The evaluation programme for this purpose will include:

- The objectives of the programme used for planned outcomes and unplanned effects.
- The procedure used for achieving the defined objectives. This also includes input to system such as teaching staff, performance of students in the classroom, facilities, instructional material and methods, technology and measurement procedure.
- The analysis of (b) as above, a plan for making a decision based on the analysis.

We have already studied the objectives of teacher education programme in other chapters. We have also studied the objectives of teacher education programme of different universities in a section of this lesson. Thus, for evaluation of the effectiveness of a teacher education programme, one has to identify objectives very precisely and assess accurately the extent to which they have been achieved.

At present, the emphasis in evaluation of effectiveness of teacher education programme is on how it has helped a person to be a good teacher. In future, we may expect from a teacher education programme to help a candidate develop as a teacher with unique talents and prepare him for an effective and appropriate role in the society.

For example, the first objective in the Teacher Education Programme at secondary level of different universities is to develop awareness among student teachers about the role of education in building up a democratic, secular, and socialistic pattern of society. Method of explicit rationale is to be used to assess the achievement of this objective. The phrases used in the objective are 'development of awareness', 'role of education', and 'democratic, secular and socialistic pattern of society.' Further, these phrases are comprised of technical terms like democracy, secular, and socialistic with reference to society.

The knowledge of these terms at the awareness level, with reference to role of education in building such a society, is to be acquired by the trainee. No one has to devise a rationale in which description of specific behaviour is to be observed or assessed in accordance with the objective. The behaviour is to be further analysed to assess its components. The evaluator has to plan a procedure for the assessment of the behaviour or its components. The level of this objective is awareness, hence the knowledge of the directed pattern of society and the role of education in achieving it in terms of degree, will indicate success or failure of the achievement of this objective.

The evaluation of the student teachers should be done with reference to:

- The skills acquired by them in terms of their achievement to practice these skills into classroom situation.
- The appropriateness of the content and pedagogical theory and instructional method.
- The effectiveness of the faculty of teacher education college in helping student teachers to achieve the objectives of teacher education programme.

- The extent to which student teachers are given an opportunity to develop a sense of responsibility for their behaviour in the classroom, will determine the effectiveness of a teacher education programme.

The teacher educators need to think about addition or deletion of the content or topic. The weightage given to different components like practice teaching, work experience, etc. should be reviewed continuously to know their contribution in development of skills, attitudes and interest. The teacher educators should continuously evaluate student teachers throughout the year. If need be, reference of topics should be modified to achieve the objectives. Otherwise, teacher educators, in consultation with curriculum experts, can recommend to the university for modification of curriculum.

The student teachers should be motivated to make efforts for learning. New areas of learning are to be added to the programme; certain areas should be given more emphasis. This is required for the modification of the programme.

The result of evaluation may be interpreted to determine the extent to which objectives are being realised. The objectives should be modified or reformulated in the light of evaluation. Hence, the entire programme should be geared to the right type of objectives and their realisation.

Evaluate Yourself

(1) What are the components to be evaluated for the effectiveness of the teacher education programme?

(2) What has been emphasized in the evaluation of the teacher education programme at present?

(3) How should student teachers be evaluated for effectiveness of the programme?

SUMMARY

1. A teacher education programme is most effective if it produces effective teachers.
2. Through evaluation, we can determine the effectiveness of teaching and success of a programme.

3. The evaluation influences teaching learning process, curriculum development, and research.
4. Therefore, evaluation should be objective, valid, reliable, comprehensive, continuous, flexible and cooperative.
5. All the three types of evaluation—preparative, formative and summative are to be used by teacher educators, planners and curriculum experts to determine the effectiveness of teacher education programme.
6. Evaluation helps in taking administrative, counselling, research and classroom decisions.
7. The purpose of evaluation of a programme is improvement, maintenance or termination.
8. Objectives of teacher education programme determine teacher learning process, learning outcomes and evaluation.
9. The effectiveness of the teacher education programme is judged in terms of objectives and procedure used for achieving the objectives.
10. The evaluation of the student teachers is also an indication of the effectiveness of the teacher education programme.

MODEL ANSWERS

1. (i) Effective teacher is a unique human being who has learned to use himself effectively and efficiently to carry out his own and society's purpose in education of their students.

   (ii) Effective teaching (by a teacher) produces maximum learning outcomes among students.

   (iii) There are two major components of effective teacher education programme:

   (a) Curriculum prescribed by the university.

   (b) Curriculum transaction carried out in a teacher training institute.

2. (i) The purposes of evaluation are:

(a) to collect evidence to show the degree of progress towards curricular goals.

(b) to enable teacher educators to know about effectiveness of teaching, experience, activities, instructional methods and materials.

(ii) Measurement is quantitative estimation of change in behaviour.

(iii) Educational evaluation is a systematic process used for determining the success of objectives. Evaluation should be:

(a) objective, (b) valid, (c) reliable, (d) comprehensive, (e) continuous, (f) flexible, (g) cooperative

3. (i) The preparative evaluation is carried out to know the input required for the effectiveness of a programme.

(ii) The formative evaluation is carried out to know the effectiveness of teaching learning during the process.

(iii) The summative evaluation is carried out at the completion of a programme.

4. (i) Purposes of programme evaluation are:

(a) Improvement of a programme

(b) Maintenance of a programme

(c) Termination of a programme

(ii) Educational decisions influenced by programme evaluation:

(a) Change or modification of curriculum

(b) Change in plan and practices

(c) Grade placement and promotion of subjects

(d) Change in self concept

(e) Effectiveness of an educational programme

(iii) Types of Educational Decisions:

(a) Administrative decisions

(b) Counselling decisions

(c) Research decisions

(d) Classroom decisions

5. (i) Three steps involved in teaching learning process:
   (a) Outcome of learning
   (b) Planning of learning experiences
   (c) Evaluation
   (ii) Criteria for planning a teacher education programme are:
   (a) Expectations of the society from teachers
   (b) The attitude towards teaching
   (c) Skills essential to carry out responsibilities of teaching
   (d) Value orientation
6. (i) Components to be evaluated for the effectiveness of the teacher education programme are:
   (a) Objectives of the programme
   (b) Procedure used for achieving the objectives
   (ii) At present, the emphasis in evaluation of the teacher education programme is on how it has helped a person to be a good teacher.
   (iii) The student teacher should be evaluated with reference to:
   (a) skills acquired by them
   (b) appropriateness of the content and pedagogical theory and instructional method
   (c) effectiveness of the faculty of teacher education college
   (d) the opportunity to develop a sense of responsibility in classroom

KEYWORDS

Measurement: Measurement is quantitative estimation of change in behaviour.

Evaluation: Evaluation is value judgement and is based on objectives.

Preparative Evaluation: Preparative evaluation is carried out to know the input required for the effectiveness of a programme.

Formulative Evaluation: Formulative evaluation is carried out to know the effectiveness of teaching learning during the process.

Summative Evaluation: Summative evaluation is carried out at the completion of the programme.

Effective Teaching: The teaching which produces maximum learning outcomes among students.

REFERENCES

Allen, Dwight and Ryan, Kevin (1969). Microteaching Mass: Addison—Wesley.

Bloom, B.S. and et al. (1971). *Handbook on Formative and Summative Evaluation of Student Learning*. New York: McGraw Hill Book Co.

Combs, Arther W. (1965). *The Professional Education of Teachers: A Perceptual View of Teacher Education*. Boston: Allyn and Bacon.

NSSE (1969). Educational Evaluation: New Roles, New Means. The Sixty-eight Year Book: Chicago: National Society for the Study of Education.

Nunnally, Jum C. (1964). *Educational Measurement and Evaluation*. New York: McGraw Hill Book Co.

Singh, L.C. (Ed.) (1990). *Teacher Education in India: A Resource Book*. New Delhi: NCERT.

Singh, Pritam (Ed.) (1986). *Evaluation at the Elementary Stage—A Book of Readings*. New Delhi: NCERT.

FURTHER READINGS

Dandekar, W.N. (1971). *Evaluation in Schools,* Shri Vidya Prakashan, Pune, Maharashtra.

Davis, I.K. (1971). *The Management of Learning*, McGraw Hills Books Co., London.

Glaser, R. and Nitko, A.J. (1971). Measurement in Learning and Instruction (in R.L. Thorndike (Ed.): *Educational Measurement* 2nd Ed. American Council of Education, Washington D.C.).

Good, C.V. (Ed. 1995). *Dictionary of Education*, McGraw Hill Book Co., New York.

Gupta, A.K. (1988). *Teacher Education*, Sterling Publishers, New Delhi.

Hough, J.B. and Duncan, J.K. (1970). *Teaching: Description and Analysis*, Addison Wesley, California.

Kundu, G.L. (1988). *Indian Year Book on Teacher Education*, Sterling Publication, New Delhi.

Mehta, C.S. and Joshi, D.C. (1973). *Principles and Problems of Teacher Education*, Part I and II (in Hindi), Rajasthan Hindi Grantha Academy Jaipur, Rajasthan.

Sharma, R.A. (1980). *Technology of Teaching: Teaching Behaviour*, Loyal Book, Depot, Meerut.

Shukla, R.S. (1989). *Shikshak Shiksha: Dasha Evam Disha* (in Hindi); Akshat Prakashan, Udaipur, Rajasthan.

Chapter 5

Professionalization of Teacher Education

STRUCTURE OF CHAPTER

INTRODUCTION

The aim of this chapter is to realize the professionalization of the teaching profession and to provide an opportunity to see the role of professional organisations and associations in raising level or quality of education.

MEANING OF PROFESSION, PROFESSIONALIZATION AND PROFESSIONALISM

Teachers—at least some of them—are walking up and insisting on being heard; they are commenting and seeking attention on problems and issues. They are beginning to demand their right to participate and even make (dictate) decisions about their welfare, educational programmes and their professional training. This exertion, as a lobby, is an indication of their becoming professionals.

Before going ahead, let us understand some related terms.

Profession—a term used to denote an ideal or typical model of an occupational organization (which may not be existing anywhere like the ideal).

Many definitions have been suggested from time to time; they vary in their degree of emphasis on the different functions that a profession is supposed to perform. According to Carr-Saunders, a profession emerges when "a number of persons are found to be practicing a definite technique founded upon a specialized training." He goes on to further define it as "an occupation based upon specialized intellectual study and training". He goes on to further define it as "an occupation based upon specialized intellectual study and training with the purpose of supplying skilled service or advice to others for a definite fee or salary". Tawney, on the other hand, defines a profession as "a trade which is organized, incompletely, no doubt, but genuinely, for the performance of a function", giving no importance to specialized knowledge or training. Lieberman, on the other hand, considers the functions of a profession as important and, in fact, is of the view that they are of two types—for their practitioners enabling them to earn a livelihood and those 'for society'. There are some who, besides attaching importance to knowledge and expertise, emphasise the necessity for unity and solidarity among the practitioners.

> **Professionalization**—the observed movement, within occupations, towards change in certain characteristics in a direction to form an occupational organization (profession).
>
> **Professionalism**—An ideology for value and related activities that can be found in many and different occupational groups wherein members aspire for professional status. Professionalism may be a necessary component of professionalization, but professionalism is not an adequate basis for the professional process.

All occupations can be placed on a continuum indicating those that meet the fewest characteristics to those that meet the most. Hence, probably, medical personnel and lawyers would fall at one end of the continuum, with unskilled labour at the other end.

A professional possesses knowledge which a layman does not possess. As an occupation becomes more professionalized, it gains in income, power and prestige, and in the process gains more control over its licensing, training, legislation and can therefore demand better quality of students for enrolment. While legal or administrative control exists in all professions, non-legal norms enforced by the profession are far more binding. A professional association provides a group identity, as it uses the colleagues as references in the conduct of work and life too. A profession is a lifelong work as rarely does a professional changes the field of work.

Questions which are repeatedly asked: Is teaching really a profession? Do teachers meet the characteristics of professionals?

CHARACTERISTICS OF A PROFESSION

To be able to generate thinking on such issues, it is essential to first identify all the characteristics of a profession. It is only then that teaching can be examined. From the various attempts to define a profession, as many as thirteen characteristics have been identified:

- Based on scientific theory.
- Service orientation.
- Functions.
- Determination of standards of education and training.
- Far-reaching adult socialization experience than in other occupation.
- Professional practice often legally recognized by some form of license.
- Boards of licensing as well as management in the hands of members of that profession.
- Occupation gains in income, power and prestige ranking and can demand higher calibre students.
- Its legislation shaped by its members.

- Practitioner comparatively free to lay evaluation and control.
- Norms of practice enforced by the profession more stringent than legal controls.
- Members are strongly identified and affiliated to the profession.
- Most probably is a terminal occupation.

Now let us see how far teaching adheres:

With regards to dealing with scientific knowledge, a teacher deals with knowledge but not necessarily scientific. In fact, most often the methods of teaching is based on their own experience, probably because of the absence of agreement on the body of essential knowledge a teacher should have; not only should there be a body of knowledge in an occupation, the citizens must acknowledge the same. The lack of this body of knowledge is the major hurdle in teacher professionalization.

Teachers satisfy the characteristic of service orientation than many others. Teachers claim that they do an important service to students and society. Teachers, social workers and nurses were strongly professionalized; however, they lack any orientation in faulty selection and training.

There is a considerable difference in the functions of education—for the development of the individual and to establish institutions that will enable an individual to develop his capabilities in light of his experiences. More recently, the functions of general education and that of vocational education have been quite different because of their emphasis at different stages of school learning–minimum levels or mastery learning. Such debates are not conducive for professionalization of teaching. The problem is that rather than the educators more laymen are not agreeing on the functions of education.

With regards to standards of education and training, teachers have no say. A whole host of institutions and agencies, with considerable diversity, determine the standards. Talking of teachers—many of you would probably agree to that, most teacher training programmes are not adequate and are redundant with no relation to classroom situations.

Most teacher training programmes are of such a short time duration that teachers go through a rather limited adult socialization period in teaching as compared with other professions.

Teachers need training/certificate/degrees to become qualified to teach. This is to ensure that the unskillful can be kept out and good candidates can be included, just as members of other professions do. In fact, teachers do not comprehend why and how they need to control entry into the profession; this is indicative of their own indifference/ignorance or naivete towards professionalism.

Linking policies and thrusts to provisions of legal approval, delays the process of change, reduces decentralization and flexibility, and tends to doubt the integrity/competence of educationists. Though teachers' salaries have increased, they have not increased in proportion to others hence many teachers tend to seek other occupations. Though strikes have increased, it is not in the same proportion as others. Therefore the lower power and prestige position tend to continue and cannot draw students of high calibre. The students drawn from homes of limited opportunities for intellectual and cultural development, have an effect on the overall quality of educational services.

Evaluation and control is significant, as the parents feel that they can evaluate the teacher through the child. The parents and the community are not the only influence that reduces teachers' authority, the teachers also do not have complete control over their students. The teacher's relationship to society reveals his lack of control, he teaches that what he is told to teach.

Teachers have norms, which are no lesser than the established professions but most of the norms are enforced by non-teachers. Teachers treat teaching as a job rather than a career. Unskilled workers shift from one job to another and the professionals remain in one.

Teacher education is a part of the profession of teaching. Clearly laid down programmes for preparation of teacher educators are not anywhere in the world and many of them consider themselves trained to become secondary teachers. As regards 'identity' of this group, it is not distinct, however they are interchangeable within the state service to administration of schools, i.e. inspectors, education officers and the like.

Teacher education has progressed considerably and several specializations have developed, however, many generalizations still exist. In fact, the controversy further widens as to whether education is a discipline or a profession.

PROFESSIONAL ORGANIZATIONS OF TEACHERS

As already discussed, the characteristic of a profession is the formation and running of a well-knit association for its practitioners, an activity of which is to collectively work for the quality of the professional service. Carr-Saunders has described the role of professional organizations as three fold: (i) to guarantee professional competence, (ii) to guarantee professional conduct of its members, and (iii) to raise the status of the profession.

Professional organizations of teachers are in a position, to have the set-up, through which teachers can, as a group, do what is not possible individually for ensuring quality of service. Further, the quality teaching by the teachers depends on the extent to which the needs of its practitioners (teachers) are met. The basic needs of all teachers can broadly be categorised as:

(i) the philosophic or professional need of a teacher to be heard on matters of importance to him like, courses, methodology, examination and evaluation as with experience, he might have evolved a thing or a strategy which he/she considers worth sharing with others for their consideration.

(ii) the need for economic security and satisfactory conditions of work by every teacher.

(iii) the ethical needs of a teacher imply protection from professional elements with the teaching profession against whom a single teacher or a minority cannot do anything else.

(iv) the need for public recognition and acceptance is a need of a teacher which he/she can get among his colleagues.

The official stance or statements by the collective group or spokesmen of a teachers' association can effectively communicate to the concerned, the need for relevant educational policies, for better salaries and improved conditions of work, creating climate for expected behaviour and enforce code of ethics in the organization, that enable a teacher to gain recognition among peers, government and public. It is this group stand that only a professional organization of teachers or an association can work towards the upliftment of quality, status, recognition and conditions.

Teachers' associations can be differentiated from professional organizations/associations of teachers by the objectives. The objective of the former may vary depending on the group they enfold. For instance, area specialized associations trade union to defend the economic interests; social and cultural associations for leisure time activity, the later, professional organizations of teachers include all the functions different associations try to achieve, professional organizations of teachers have the interests of the teacher at heart and work with the objective of ensuring quality of professional service.

Hence, the success may be looked at how far it has succeeded in professionalizing teaching, by controlling qualifications of entrants in order to improve the quality of teaching and at the same time pushing for a better work ethos. In other words, by setting standards for the profession and ensuring that they are enforced with regards to the entry, professional practice-teaching at the teacher training institutes, research with a view—to adding to knowledge, which should determine the functioning of the profession.

Although a professional organisation of teachers has no direct control over the teacher training institutions in the area, they try to influence entry into the profession at training or employment level, programme of study or even certification.

Activities of professional organisations have some commonality, however, the type and number taken up depends on its leadership, status, finances at its disposal. The common activities are annual conferences usually with a theme, publications comprising periodicals, year books, reports, undertaking and commissioning research of information, laison with related institutions, organisations, reacting to related matter including recognition of institutions offering courses, determining and controlling professional and other behaviour of its members.

The membership of professional organisations of teachers varies from an annual to life membership—individual, institutional, and associate membership, for those who are not regular members of the profession; these are all paying membership. Renowned persons may also be honoured by being offered an honorary membership.

An organisation may be local, national or international depending on the organisation's constitution. In fact, sometimes a national organisation may even have local chapters.

Recognition and credibility of any organisation, including a professional organisation of teachers, is possible only when it registers with the Registrars of Societies. Only after that, it can bargain or fight for a cause, particularly for rights of its members.

A variety of professional organisations not directly concerned with teacher education and teaching but with specific subjects or teachers, interest teacher educators.

INTERNATIONAL ORGANISATIONS OF TEACHERS

World Confederation of Organisations of the Teaching Profession (WCOTP) is an international organisation of which any organisation of teachers can seek membership. Its first counterpart is the World Federation of Teacher Organisations to which organisations of socialist and leftist teachings can become members. Some national level organisations are the American Federation of Teachers (AFT), the National Union of Teachers (in the U.K.), Australian Teacher's Federation and the All India Federation of Education Association (AIFEA) in India.

There are specialized teacher education associations in India and abroad organisations on specific areas of education in general, as well as in special areas of teacher education. Examples of specialized associations are Indian Science Congress, Indian Social Science Congress, All India Federation of University and College Teacher's Organisation (AIFUCTO), and All India

Science Teachers Association. Examples of teacher education organisations at the international level are International Council of Education for Teaching. American Association of Colleges of Teacher Education (AACTE), and Indian Association of Teacher Educators (IATE). Some examples of those in specific areas of education are Indian Association of Pre-school Education, Indian Psychological Association, India Sociology Association, the All-India Association of Educational and Vocational Guidance, All-India Association of Educational Technology, Comparative Education Society.

Evaluate Yourself

1. List two characteristics of a profession.
2. Name two international organisations of teachers.

ALL INDIA FEDERATION OF EDUCATIONAL ASSOCIATION (AIFEA)

In the first thirty years of this century, teachers' organisations emerged in several states, but their activities were restricted to the state of their origin and they were also limited in their membership, as their parameters were the level at which they taught (primary, secondary) and the managements of the schools they worked in (private, government). There was no co-operation among them as there was no agency to coordinate their functions. The All India Federation of Teachers' Associations was formed in 1925.

The idea of a national level federation was conceived by the leaders of the teachers' movement in U.P. specifically the representatives of the U.P. Secondary Education Association, so that all teachers could come under one banner. In 1983, it was renamed as All India Federation of Educational Associations since the term 'teachers' associations' gave the impression of trade unionism because of which several academic associations were not becoming members. Now it affiliates organisations of all categories of teachers as well as associations of different subjects—All India Science Teachers Association, Indian Association of Teacher Educators, Association of Heads of Anglo Indian Schools, Delhi Public Library and the like.

Though the annual conferences held in the Christmas vacation, every year since 1925, the cause of education, which is the chief concern of the Federation has been neglected. Thousands of teachers of different cadres, representatives of teachers' organisations, educationists and administrators, assemble and discuss problems of education and the profession. The annual conferences, exhibitions, sectional conferences, memorial, lectures are held regularly.

The specific objectives of the AIFFA are:

- to promote effective programmes for the country.
- to enable exchange of information and ideas among teachers, parents, and educationists.
- to safeguard and improve the status of the teaching profession in India and to secure its legitimate place in national life by promoting among teachers, a sense of national responsibility and professional efficiency.
- to unify members of the teaching profession at all levels from the pre-primary to the university.
- to cultivate goodwill by active participation in international teachers' and educational conferences.

The AIFEA has been advocating a national pay structure, improved service conditions for teachers and their involvement in the formation of educational policies. The federation prophesises that unless certain fundamental rights and responsibilities are not passed on to teachers by the government and the society, the desired objectives of education cannot be achieved. Teacher accountability, which is still being discussed to be woven into the system was evolved as far back as in 1935. On the issue of teachers' status, it conducted two seminars on pay scales and teachers organisations, evolved a national consensus and communicated the same to the Indian Education Commission (1964-66).

At the international level, it is affiliated to the World Confederation of Organisations of the Teaching Profession (WCOTP) and also represented on National Committee for Cooperation with UNESCO. It also sought the conduct of the All Asia Education Conference, member of WCOTP, at Banaras in 1930. Again in 1961, it hosted the tenth annual conference of the W.C.O.T.P. in Delhi. In 1975, as part of its Golden Jubilee Celebrations, the discussion centred on the role of teachers' organisations in society, working of the teachers' associations, representation of teachers and service to teachers.

The Federation does not collect subscription directly from the members but from the association affiliated to it. It has an admission fee and an annual affiliation fee.

INDIAN ASSOCIATION OF TEACHER EDUCATORS (IATE)

Association of Principals of Training Colleges in India was established in 1950 as a resultant of a meeting of principals of secondary teacher training institutions; the membership being open only to institutions offering a B.Ed. With the opening of the membership to the members of the institutions, it was renamed All India Association of Training Colleges (AIATC) in 1964 and later it was renamed All India Association of Training Colleges (AIATC) in 1964. In 1965, it opened its membership to all teacher training institutions and teacher educators working at all levels its name was changed to National Association of Teacher Educators but the name had to be changed again due to the fact that the Registrar of Societies does not register any non-governmental society with the term 'national' in its name. Thus, it was called by its present name, Indian Association of Teacher Educators (IATE).

THE AIM AND OBJECTIVES OF THE IATE

- to develop and promote teacher education.
- to cooperate with other organisations and institutions which are actively working for improving teacher education.
- to provide a forum for discussion of problems related to teacher education and also to offer suggestions for measures to be taken from time to time, by the state government and affecting teacher education.
- to cooperate with other agencies working for improvement of education.

- to support, protect and improve the character, status and interests of teacher educators and to secure their legitimate place in national life by including a sense of national responsibility, professional efficiency and accepted standards of professional and social morality.

Upto 1964, its annual meetings were not held regularly; between 1964-75 it met regularly. In this period, it was a powerful body in that it was accepted by the government. National Council of Educational Research and Training (NCERT), National Council for Teacher Education (NCTE), Planning Commission, University Grant Commission (UGC) on policy making in teacher education. Like the AIFEA, it presented a draft for teacher education to the Indian Education Commission (1964-66) as a result of their conference. In fact, the draft was the major basis for the recommendations of the Commission. Similar efforts resulted in larger provision for funds in the Fourth five-year Plan and the Planning Commission included its recommendations on teacher education.

From time to time, the IATE has been extending support to ventures like the four-year integrated courses for teacher education, the National Council of Teacher Education (NCTE) as well as State Board of Teacher Education (SBTE) correspondence courses in teacher education. It has also drawn up and recommended new curricula for B.Ed. and M.Ed. courses, working through its committees, which discussed the issues at the conferences. These have even been adopted in some universities.

The first Asian Conference of Teacher Educators was organised by it in 1972; the report in its published form, is one of its good publications. It has brought out 25 publications along with Teacher Education, a journal indexed and quoted internationally.

Issues normally taken up by trade unions, like salaries of teacher educators, was not a normal stance except when demanded by members of the general meetings.

It has not been able to retain its earlier reputation as representing teacher educators and teacher education at all levels, nor of its all India character.

Earlier, office bearers were elected by the members present at the annual conference happening for the subsequent year, but with the passage of time, membership was increased and elections to the executive level through a postal ballot were introduced.

Presently, there is no agency that can collate and present view of teacher educators on issues in the area as the representative of the nation's educators. Such gaps stand in the way of effective communication of the view of practitioners.

SUMMARY

1. Organisations and associations of professional groups enable the generation to think of related issues and with the group resources and power, facilitate the effective implementation of recommendations and the consequent maintenance of standards through these inbuilt checks.

MODEL ANSWERS

(i) (a) It is based on scientific theory.

(b) Its legislation is shaped by its members.

(ii) (a) World Confederation of Organizations of the Teaching Profession (WCOTP).

(b) National Union of Teachers (U.K.).

KEYWORDS

Profession: A term used to denote an ideal or typical model of an occupational organization.

Professionalization: The observed movement within occupations, towards change in certain characteristics in a direction to form an occupational organization.

Professionalism: An ideology (or value) and related activities that can be found in many and different occupational groups wherein members aspire to professional status. Professionalism may be a necessary component of professionalization, but professionalism is not an adequate basis for the professional group.

REFERENCES

Gupta, A.K. *Teacher Education*, Sterling Publishers, New Delhi, 1988.

Khan, M.S. *Teacher Education in India and Abroad*, New Delhi: Ashish Publishing House, 1983.

Myers, Donalsa A. *Teacher Power-Professionalization and Collective Bargaining*. London: Lexington Bros., 1974.

Ruhela, S.P. ed. *Sociology of the Teaching Profession in India*, New Delhi: NCERT, 1970.

Sharma, R.A. *Teacher Education*, International Publication House, Meerut, U.P. 1986.

Sree Dharaswamy, S. *Teacher Organisations in India*, Secundrabad: All India Federation of Educational Associations 1980.

FURTHER READINGS

Barnard, H.C. (1967). *An Introduction of Teaching*, University of London Press, London.

Davis, I.K. (1971). *The Management of Learning*, McGraw-Hill Book Co. London.

De Cecco, J.P. and Grawford, W.R. (1977). *The Psychology of Learning and Instruction*, Prentice Hall Inc: Englewood Cliffs, New Jersey.

Marrison, A. and Mc Intyre, D. (1969). *Teacher and Teaching*. Armonds Worth, Penguin.

Remmers, H.H. and Gage, N.L. (1955). *Educational Measurement and Evaluation*, Harper and Brothers, New York.

Russell, D.H. (1960). Teaching for Concept Development (in C.W. Harris (Ed): *Encyclopedia of Educational Research*, The Mc Millan Co. New York.

Saxena, N.R. Mishra, B.K. and Mohanty, R.K. (1998). *Teacher Education*, R. Lall Book Depot, Meerut, U.P.

Shukla, R.S. (1978). *Emerging Trends in Teacher Education*, Chugh Publication, Allahabad (U.P.).

Singh T. and Singh P. (1983). *Shikshan Abhyas Ke Sopan* (in Hindi) Bharat Bharti. Prakashan, Husanabad Jaunpur (U.P.).

Srivastava, R.C. and Bose, K. (1973). *Theory and Practice of Teacher Education in India*, Chugh Publications, Allahabad.

Storm, R.D. (1971). *Teaching and Learning Process*, Prentice Hall Inc., Englewood Cliff, New Jersey

Thelen, H.A. (1960). *Education and the Human Quest*, Harper and Raw, New Delhi.

Chapter 6

In-service Education of Teachers

STRUCTURE OF CHAPTER

- Introduction
- Meaning and Purposes of In-service Education
  - Continuous Process
  - Purposes
  - Objectives
- Critical Appreciation of Activities of NCTE, NCERT and NIEPA
  - National Council of Teacher Education
  - National Council of Educational Research and Training (NCERT)
  - National Institute of Educational Planning and Administration (NIEPA)
- Programmes of In-service Training in Other Countries USA, UK and Russia
- Summary
- Evaluate Yourself
- References
- Further Readings

INTRODUCTION

In the earlier chapters, we have studied aims, objectives, purposes and types of teacher education. There are two important aspects of teacher preparation—pre-service or initial training and in-service or continuing education of teachers. Some of the techniques of in-service education are workshops, seminars, refresher courses, and summer schools. These are examples of personal contact mode. However, in-service education can be given through distance mode using print and non-print materials.

MEANING AND PURPOSES OF IN-SERVICE EDUCATION

The individuals before they join schools as teachers, are exposed to theoretical course in education and practice teaching normally in a college of education or a teacher training institution. Such a course leads to a degree, diploma or certificate. This is known as pre-service education of school teachers. It is a programme of activities aiming at their continuing professional growth. It is the sponsoring and pursuing of activities which will bring new insight, growth, understandings and co-operative practices to the members of the teaching profession and make them better teachers. Some of the popularly known techniques of in-service education are workshops, seminars, conferences, refresher courses and summer schools, etc.

The need and importance of in-service educators of schools teachers has been long recognised in India, especially in the post-independence period. The University Commission (1948-49) stressed that the refresher courses should be organised for high school and intermediate college teachers. The Secondary Education Commission (1952-53) emphasised the need for the provision of refresher courses, practical training in workshops and seminars and professional conferences for school teachers. The National Commission on Teachers-I (1985) has recommended that each teacher needs to be provided in-service education in every cycle of five years. The National Policy on Education (1986) has greatly stressed that in-service education is an inseparable part of teacher education, and wants to overhaul the system of teacher education to enable it to meet the thrust envisaged in the policy.

Continuous Process

It appears that the NPE-1986 does not recognise that pre-service and in-service education are two different types of training of teachers. These are in fact two consecutive phrases for the same process. These are on a continuum, starting with pre-service to continue till the teacher is in the teaching profession. The success of in-service education programme of school teachers, which is a continuous on-going process, depends on its acceptability to the teachers. It is generally felt that the teachers resist the idea of going in for in-service education and they take such programmes very lightly. The situation can be changed and programmes made popular among teachers, if in-service education is 'need-oriented' for teachers and if we are able to convince the teachers that all that is being done emanates from the professional needs and will go a long way to improve the educational practice.

Purpose

- To provide adequate professional training so as to make the teaching-learning effective.
- To keep the teacher abreast of new developments in curricular subjects and pedagogy.
- To upgrade the academic qualification of teachers.
- To develop the skills and attitudes responsive to emerging national development goals and programmes.
- To make the teachers aware of the problems of the community and to develop the necessary skills and attitudes which brings effective changes in the society.

Objectives

The following are the objectives of in-service education of teachers as suggested by Prof. Akhtar Siddiqui (1991):

- Providing professional training and qualifications to the untrained working teachers. There are some teachers in certain states who were appointed without any prior training for teaching. For these teachers, there is a legitimate need for providing training.
- Upgrading the qualification of in-service teachers whose original qualification may have been rendered out of date by certain changes in the educational system.
- Arranging refresher courses, particularly to familiarise teachers with modern practices, being encouraged in schools. The need to up-date teachers in production of teaching aid materials, use of audio-video aids and application of evaluation techniques, is widely felt across the country.

- Disseminating specific educational innovations, such as introduction of SUPW (Socially Useful Productive Work), population education, teacher participation in non-formal education of children in deprived sections of society, etc.
- Improving the quality of educational management and administration at all levels is an important purpose of in-service education. This may include re-training of teachers to enable them to take up new responsibilities outside the classrooms for which their earlier training and experience may not have equipped them adequately.
- Improving the quality of teacher education. There is a growing emphasis on the needs for continuing education of the teacher educators themselves.

Evaluate Yourself

1. National Commission of Teachers (1) recommended that in-service training should be provided once in ...... years.
2. Refresher courses were stressed for high school and intermediate colleges by ....
3. In-service education broadly aims at ....
4. Write any two purposes of in-service education, each in five lines.
5. Write in brief (in five lines) the need for guidance.

CRITICAL APPRECIATION OF ACTIVITIES OF NCTE, NCERT AND NIEPA

The in-service education of teachers is generally organised by several agencies and institutions. There are agencies at the national level, such as National Council for Teacher Education (NCTE), National Council for Educational Research and Training (NCERT), National Institute of Educational Planning and Administration (NIEPA), Central Board of Secondary Education (CBSE), and Central Institute of Educational Technology (CIET), which organise in-service education and training programmes for educational personnel of different categories, viz. administrators, supervisors, teachers, teacher educators, and subject specialists, etc. Similarly, there are agencies at the state level which are responsible for in-service education programmes within the State. These are: State Councils of Educational Research and Training (SCERTs), State Council of Science Education (SCSEs), and State Institute of Educational Technology (SIETs). At the district and institutional level, the in-service education programmes for teachers and teacher educators are organised by institutions like District Institutes of Education and Training (DIETs), Colleges of Teacher Education (CTEs), Institutes of Advanced Studies in Education (IASEs), Extension Service Developments or Centres attached to Colleges of Education, and University Departments of Education and School complexes.

However, there are school systems which conduct such programmes for their own teachers, for example, Kendriya Vidyalaya Sangathan (KVS), and Navodaya Vidyalaya Samiti (NVS). The set of schools under the semi-private management also conduct in-service education programmes for teachers of their schools during summer and winter vacations. Some large schools have school-based training programmes for their teachers.

In the following pages, the role and functioning of NCTE, NCERT and NIEPA will be briefly described and critical appreciation of the programmes and activities of these national level organisations will be made.

National Council of Teacher Education (NCTE)

NCTE was established in 1973 by a resolution of the Ministry of Education, Government of India for maintaining standards in teacher education. The Union Ministry of Education is the ex-officio president of NCTE and the director NCERT is the member-secretary. There are 42 members of the council consisting of one representative from each State, University Grants Commission (UGC), All India Council for Technical Education (AICTE), Central Advisory Board of Education (CABE), Planning Commission, NCERT and 12 experts in the field of school, technical and vocational, teacher education, nominated by the President. The NCTE has its general body whose president is the Union Ministry of Human Resource Development. Steering Committee whose Chairman is the member-secretary, NCTE and three Academic Standing Committees whose chairpersons, are the experts in the concerned fields.

While the academic standing committees may meet more often to discuss issues and problems concerning teacher's education, the council meets once a year to consider the recommendations of the Standing Committees and to give broad guidelines and recommendations on matters of policy. Academic programmes such as curriculum development preparation of curricular materials and evaluation for teacher educators conducted through workshops, seminars, orientation programmes, are organised in pursuance of the recommendations made by the NCTE. Although NCTE is a sort of 'Think Tank' in teacher education, it's role at present is advisory. However, some members of the Council felt the need for giving statutory status to NCTE as the National Policy on Education (1986) and also the modified NPE-1992 has also recommended for conferring statutory status in the NCTE. Unless the NCTE becomes the statutory body by an Act of Parliament it is difficult to implement its recommendations pertaining to setting up maintenance and quality of teacher education, both preservice and in-service throughout the country.

National Council of Educational Research and Training (NCERT)

NCERT was established in New Delhi on 1 September 1961 for providing academic support in improving the quality of school education in India. It is the academic adviser to the Ministry of Human Resource Development (HRD) of the Government of India. The Ministry draws upon NCERT's expertise while formulating and implementing policies and programmes in the areas of school and teacher education. NCERT is an autonomous body and is registered under the Societies Registration Act (1860).

The functions of the NCERT broadly rotate to: (a) research and development, (b) in-service and pre-service training, and (c) extension and dissemination work—all these tuned to achieve the main objective of improving the quality of school education. The NCERT, therefore (i) develops curriculum, instructional and exemplar materials, methods of teaching techniques of evaluation, teacher aids, kits and equipment learning resources, etc. (ii) organises pre-service training of teachers, teacher educators and other resources, etc. (iii) organises pre-service and in-service training of teachers, teacher educators and other educational personnel, (iv) conducts, and promotes educational research, (v) disseminate improved educational techniques and practices and research findings, and (vi) acts as a clearing house for ideas and information on all matters relating to school education and teacher education.

The NCERT functions through six constituent units, namely (a) National Institute of Education (NIE), (b) Central Institute of Educational Technology (CIET)—both located in New Delhi and four Regional Institutes of Education (RIEs) at Ajmer, Bhopal, Bhubaneshwar and Mysore. The National Institute of Education organises activities related to: (a) research and development, (b) in-service training, and (c) publishing and dissemination programmes. Important among these programmes are development and evaluation of curriculum, instructional materials, learning resources and instructional strategies.

Though NIE primarily confines its activities to in-service training but, yet conducts a regular nine-month diploma course in educational and vocational guidance. Is it possible that the NIE can conduct in-service courses of various kinds for teachers of different stages of school education? Since there are about 62 lacs school teachers in the country, it would take decades to cover all the teachers under the in-service education programmes. The NIE, therefore, trains key personnel at the state level who in-turn resource personnel for the in-service courses.

The NIE also develops instructional material for use by the states. The material is translated in their respective languages and published for use in the in-service courses. In addition to NIE, in-service courses for teachers are regularly conducted by the RIEs in their respective regions. Although in-service education has been organised in the country since the establishment of All India Council for Secondary Education in 1958 which later was merged into NCERT, there has not been any national system or model of in-service education of school teachers. There is a need for the development a functional model of in-service education.

National Institute of Educational Planning and Administration (NIEPA)

In 1970, the National Staff College for Educational Planner and Administrators was renamed as National Institute of Educational Planning and Administration. Following are some of its objectives as given in the document of its registration:

(i) To organise pre-service and in-service training. conferences, meetings, seminars and briefing sessions for senior educational officers of the central and state governments and union territories.

(ii) To organise orientation, training programmes and refresher courses for teacher educators and for universities and college administrators connected with educational planning and administrators.

(iii) To organise orientation programme, seminars and discussion groups for top level persons including legislators in the field of educational planning and administration at policy level in Central and State Governments.

(iv) To undertake, aid, promote and co-ordinate research in various aspects of educational planning and administration, including comparative studies in planning techniques and administrative procedures in the different States of India and in other countries of the world.

(v) To provide academic and professional guidance to agencies, institutions and personnel engaged in educational planning and administration.

(vi) To offer, on request, consultative services to state governments and other educational institutions.

(vii) To act as a clearing house of ideas and information in research, training and extension in educational planning and administration services and other programmes.

The NIEPA, therefore, organises in-service training to a good number of school principals who are involved in planning and school management and to district education officers, who are involved in district level planning and supervision of school education. In order to clear the backlog of untrained educational administrators, NIEPA has also resorted to the distance education strategy. Some correspondence-cum-contact programmes in educational planning and administration have already been organised. The programme has been developed into an additional medium of in-service training which is expected to complement its short term and seminar/workshop programmes.

Now NIEPA is working as a National University of Educational Planning and Administration (NUEPA).

Evaluate Yourself

Put a tick (✓) against the correct response.

1.	CBSE organises in-service education programmes for university teachers.	T	F
2.	CIET is an independent government organisation.	T	F
3.	SCSE is a state level organisation for improvement of science education	T	F
4.	NCTE does not organise in-service training courses for school teachers.	T	F
5.	NCERT generally organises training programmes for key persons at state level for in-service courses for teachers.	T	F

PROGRAMMES OF IN-SERVICE TRAINING IN OTHER COUNTRIES—U.S.A., U.K. AND RUSSIA

Most of the nations in the world face identical problems in the development of their educational system. If comparative problems of education are looked into, it may be possible to deduce lessons from the achievement and mistakes of other countries. The valuable experience and lessons in the improvement may be used them with reference to reorientation of the education system of one's own country. In this light, the experiences of programmes of in-service training in other countries, specially in U.S.A., U.K. and Russia are being discussed in this chapter.

U.S.A.

In U.S.A. the practice of in-service education of teachers comes almost side by side with the pre-service teacher training. The rationales for in-service education are that the teacher should continue to grow intellectually, although during the four years of teacher preparation in teacher education college; he is not adequately prepared and he is yet to learn more. He needs to be kept abreast with new developments in his subject. Majority of the in-service programmes for continuing education are conducted by members of the faculty of college of education or university departments in mornings, early afternoons or evenings, or on Saturdays and Sundays. Some programmes are arranged in summer vacations. Even some private metropolitan institutions are realising that part time instruction of teacher's in-service is paying and they run some courses in education. Some school boards depute their meritorious teachers to attend more in-service courses so that they could become better teachers.

Some universities run "On Campus" or extension courses conducted by competent persons of the faculty. Primary school teachers earn more credits in formal education for certification as secondary school teachers and they will stay on in primary school only for a higher salary. School boards do consider a teacher more competent if he has taken a few more courses. Conant recommended that one should be allowed to add to one's credit if he does masters courses in summer sessions, which increases his competence. For some summer sessions, the teacher should have financial assistance and leave, with salary. A senior teacher in a secondary school may move up in a graduate school of education after completing his summer courses. No credit should be given for "On Campus" or for extension courses.

However, it is realised that in-service education is to be a planned programme for improving the competency of teachers.

U.K.

James report (1968) recommended that a large number of teachers should be released for in-service training after every seven years. Thus constituted third cycle, an important part of their recommendation. However, in effect, nearly three per cent are being released for this training and surely a teacher would take more than seven years to get another change.

During this period, teacher can acquire higher qualifications as well and thereby qualify for higher positions in colleges or the inspectorate. The university departments of education, colleges of education, etc. offer these courses. The Council for National Academy Awards also provides a variety of programmes of varying duration.

The basic idea behind the present efforts is to see that the teachers at all levels in school's system have graduate degrees and are provided with regular facilities for training. Around 500 centres have been opened where teachers can come for studying curriculum developments.

Russia

Teachers are provided opportunities for professional growth in various ways within the school. A teacher has to undergo a training course at fixed intervals of time in order to be entitled to an increment in salary. A teacher has to go for in-service training regularly. The duration of these courses is now of one month. Major in-service courses are of two months duration. Teachers working in towns attend the weekend courses by coming to the centres once a week.

The in-service training institutions form a network. Every autonomous region has an in-service training institution. Also, every district has pedagogical centres. In 1982, there were 90 in-service training institutions and 3000 pedagogical centers. The institutes for teacher improvement provide courses for upgrading the subject knowledge of teachers, help them to solve their classroom problems and stimulate the urge for professional growth in them. The experience of other teachers is made available to them with a view to "Strengthening the ties of the school with life."

Recently, considerable attention has been paid to the advanced training of teachers. Once in five years, on an average, every teacher updates his qualifications at refresher courses organised at higher educational establishments. About 70,000 school teachers and other educational workers attend these courses. Specific curricula and syllabi have been drawn up for teachers' refresher courses. The content of these courses varies, depending upon the background of these trainees. Theoretical courses are supplemented with practical familiarisation with achievements in science and advanced work methods. Independent study during the periods between sessions is an important feature of the system. Russia has also introduced the institutions for helping teachers, headmasters and supervisors to improve their skills.

SUMMARY

1. In-service education of school teachers is a programme of activities aiming at their continuous professional growth through workshops, seminars, refresher courses and summer schools.
2. In-service education starts the day teacher joins his teaching profession and continues till the teacher is in the profession.
3. The programmes of 'in-service education has to be need-based'.
4. They should meet the professional needs of the teacher.
5. The main purpose is to make teachers more competent in their main task of teaching and improve pupil learning.
6. There are several national level agencies like NUEPA and NCRET, etc. which plan, design and implement in-service education and training programmes for school teachers in collaboration with state level agencies—S.C.E.R.T., S.C.S.E., S.I.E.T. and institutions like IASEs, C.T.Es., and D.I.E.Ts.

7. The experiences of U.S.A., U.K., and Russia in the area of in-service education show that the teacher need to be kept abreast with new developments in his subject.
8. Teachers must attend in-service education courses once in five to seven years and should be credited for promotion. Teacher centres or institutions should be set up at the regional level and possibly at district level to offer in-service programmes.

MODEL ANSWERS

1. (i) 5 years (ii) University Education Commission
   (iii) Professional development (iv) Search yourself
   (v) Search yourself
2. (i) F (ii) F (iii) T (iv) T (v) T

KEYWORDS

Pre-service Education. It is an initial training comprising of theoretical course and practice in teaching, undertaken before entering into the teaching profession viz., B.Ed. JBT, etc.

In-service Education. It is a programme of activities aiming at continuing professional growth of teachers.

REFERENCES

Buch, M.B. and Palasane, M.M. (1968). *Reading in In-service Education*, Sardar Patel University, Vallabha Vidyanagar.

Chilkana, M.R. (1985). "Centres for Continuing Education: Functions, Provisions and Activities" Paper presented at CIET, New Delhi.

Koerner James D. (1968). *Reforms in Education*, Weldenfeld Nicolson, London.

Siddiqui, M. Akhtar (1991). *In-service Teacher Education*, Ashish Publishing House, New Delhi.

Singh, L.C. (1985). *Third National Survey of Teacher Education*, NCERT, New Delhi.

Singh, L.C. (Ed). (1990). *Teacher Education in India: A Resource Book*; NCERT, New Delhi.

Singh, L.C. and Malhotra, S.P. (1992). Trend Report on Teacher Education in Fourth Survey of Research in Education by M.B. Buch, NCERT.

FURTHER READINGS

Bellack, A.A. et. al. (1966). The Language of Classroom Teachers' College Press Columbia.

Bhattacharya, G.S. (1990). *Teacher Education*, Vinod Pustak Mandir, Agra.

Bloom, B.S. (1963). *Historical Examples of Teaching Methods*, in N.L. Gage (Ed.). *Handbook of Research on Teaching*, Rand, McNally & Co. Chicago.

Challenges of Education Policy Perspectives (1985). Ministry of Human Resource Development, Govt. of India, New Delhi

Deway, J. (1916). *Democracy and Education*, MacMillan Book, Co., New York.

Glatter, R. and Wedell, E.H. (1971). *Study of Correspondence*, Longmans, London.

Green, T.F. (1971). *The Activities of Teaching*, McGraw Hill Book Co. New York.

Gupta, A.K. (1988). *Teacher Education*, Sterling Publications, New Delhi.

Herbart, J.F. (1904). *Outlines of Educational Doctrine*, Macmillan book Co. New York.

Kundu, C.L. (1988). *Indian Year book on Teacher Education*, Sterling Publications, New Delhi.

Resource Book on Teacher Education (1990). NCERT, Publication, NCERT Sri Aurobindo Marg, New Delhi.

Chapter 7

Recent Trends in Teacher Education

STRUCTURE OF CHAPTER

- Introduction
- Content of Teacher Education Curriculum
  - Greater Emphasis on Practicum
  - Training of Teachers in Special Education
  - Emerging Areas of Teacher Education
- Transactional Approaches
  - Learner Centred Approach
  - Teaching Strategies
  - Acquisition of Teaching Skills
- Increasing use of Electronic Gadgets
- Resurgence of Interest in Action Research
- Transaction of Common Core Components
- Maintenance of Standards of Teacher Education
- Four Year Integrated Course in Teacher Education
- Centralised Admission Test
- Summary
- Evaluate Yourself
- Keywords
- References
- Further Readings

INTRODUCTION

We have already studied the need for education of teachers, curricula of teacher education programmes, importance of in-service education of teachers, etc. in the earlier chapters.

In this chapter, we would study the recent trends in teacher education programme. We are aware that changes are taking place in the objectives of school education. School Curriculum has undergone revision due to changes in objectives of school education and explosion of knowledge. Changes in methods of teaching in the classroom are also taking place due to findings of researches conducted in this area. As a result of these changes, content and process of teacher education curriculum is undergoing suitable changes. We would learn about recent trends in the content and process of teacher education curricula in the following paragraphs:

CONTENT OF TEACHER EDUCATION CURRICULUM

Curricula of teacher education programmes are undergoing changes to make the programme more functional, as existing curricula are quite outdated. Prospective teachers acquire knowledge and skills which are of very limited value to them for functioning as effective classroom practitioners.

There is now greater emphasis on practicum, training of teachers in special education, etc. A number of new areas have emerged. There is a demand for incorporation of these areas in the teacher education programmes. These trends are discussed in brief in the following paragraphs.

Greater Emphasis on Practicum

Earlier in the teacher education programme, an emphasis was laid on theoretical aspects. Prospective teachers were therefore provided more of theoretical knowledge. Real experiences of classroom activities were very limited. Now, the trend is to attach greater importance to practicum/field work. The practicum/field work consists of the following two components:

(i) Internship searching including field assignments

(ii) Practical work including working with community, social work and work experience

In the teacher education curricula developed by the NCERT for teacher education, programmes for both the levels—secondary teacher education and elementary teacher education, the weightage to foundation course is only 20%. The weightage for practicum field work is 40%. This clearly reflects that a greater emphasis is now being laid on practicum/field work.

Training of Teachers in Special Education

The attainment of universalization of elementary education is a constitutional directive. Children with disabilities—physical and mental, constitute a sizeable section of school going population. Children with severe disabilities are taught in specialised institutions. During the last few years, a number of research studies have been conducted. These studies have amply demonstrated that children with mild disabilities are best educated in the company of normal children in general schools.

Besides, a large body of knowledge concerning methods and techniques of integrated education-of children with mild disabilities in general schools has been developed. Every teacher is now required to deal with children with mild disabilities in his class. He therefore, needs to be equipped with knowledge of the disabilities of children and necessary skills to handle these children. This component is therefore, being included in teacher education programme, both at the elementary and secondary level.

Special education is also an elective paper in the teacher education for both the levels-elementary and secondary teacher education. Some universities have also started courses like B.Ed. (Special Education) and M.Ed. (Special Education).

Emerging Areas of Teacher Education

There has been a phenomenonal increase in the knowledge relating to the discipline of education over the last few decades. As a result, a number of new areas for study have emerged. There is a claim for these emerging areas to be placed into the curriculum of teacher education programme. Some of these areas are mentioned below:

1. Futurology in Education
2. Special Education for the Disabled
3. Population Education
4. Family Life Education
5. Consumer Education

6. Safety Education
7. Non-formal Education
8. Adult Education
9. Educational Technology
10. International Education
11. Multigrade Teaching
12. Guidance & Counselling
13. Value Education
14. Productivity Education
15. Computer Literacy & Computer Assisted Instruction
16. Women Education

Of the areas mentioned above, some have already been introduced in the teacher education curriculum. The claim of other areas is likely to be considered by curriculum committees in the coming 10 to 15 years. Some of them may manage to find a place.

Evaluate Yourself

1. Mention the components which constitute practicum/ field work.
2. Why a greater emphasis is now laid on practicum in teacher education programme?
3. Do you consider the training of every teacher in special education essential? If yes, mention the reasons for this.
4. List five new areas which are claiming place in teacher education curriculum.

TRANSACTIONAL APPROACHES

Another trend in teacher education programme is the change in transactional approaches to the curriculum. The National Policy on Education (1986) and revised policy (1992) envisages changes in teacher's role and function. Instead of being a mere instructor, he is expected to assume the role of facilitator of learning. This role therefore, calls for a change in teaching a style from mere verbal exposition to interactive in the classroom between the teachers and pupils. It is required to organise learning situations in which learning becomes a joyful experience and the learner, instead of mere passive listener, becomes an active partner in the teaching learning process. Therefore, an emphasis is now laid on to equip prospective teacher with the following approaches to transact curriculum in the classroom.

- Learner Centred Approach
- Teaching strategies
- These approaches are discussed very briefly in the following paragraphs

Learner Centered Approach

As a teacher. We know very well that learning in most of our classrooms is not a joyful experience. Learners are the passive listeners. Their participation in the teaching learning process is very limited rather negligible. As a result, pupil's attainment in different subjects is hardly satisfactory.

In the learner centered approach, pupil is actively involved in the teaching learning process. Such involvement may be described by the phrase 'learning through participation' Perceived pupil needs are the basis for teaching. Further, the integration of cognitive and effective aspects of learning is emphasised. The main distinction between the learner centred approach and the traditional approach of teaching is not so much in the content as in the method of imparting it.

In the learner centred approach, the main function of the teacher is not so much to instruct but to evoke learning. Warm and supportive climate is emphasised. This is essential for helpful for a child to feel at home in the classroom. The clear-cut distinction between curricular and co-curricular activities that exists in the traditional approach does not exist in the learner centered approach. Learner centred approach does not mean zero teacher direction. It envisages varying degrees of teacher direction depending upon instructional objectives. The main characteristics of learner centred approach are giving stress on knowing the child, emphasis on developing learning skills, learning a joyful experience, learners' active participation, learning through activities, etc.

Teaching Strategies

We are aware that a great deal of emphasis in the teacher education programme is laid on teaching prospective teacher leaning theories—the process of how learners learn. It has been the conviction that if prospective teacher properly understands the learning theories, they can always act upon them for teaching effectively in the classroom.

It is now being realised that teaching and learning are different processes. Whereas learning theories explain as to how learning takes place, teaching theories ought to explain as to how an individual should induce another individual to learning so that the former is able to optimize learning on the latter's part.

We may be knowing that scholars have recently begun to reject the folklore that teaching skill is inborn. It is now increasingly being realised that teaching can be studied objectively with successful instructional approaches and strategies can be identified and taught. Though theories of teaching are yet to be developed by researchers, many researchers have identified teaching strategies which have been found to be quite useful in promoting better learning. These teaching strategies are inquiry training, concept attainment, advance organiser, inductive thinking, biological science inquiry, cognitive growth, etc. A great emphasis is now being laid to provide experiences to prospective teachers to help them to acquire these transactional approaches, so that they may transact the curriculum in the classroom effectively. We would read in details about these transactional approaches in paper on Education Technology.

Acquisition of Teaching Skills

An emphasis is now being laid on equipping the prospective teachers with teaching skills through micro-teaching approach. A number of studies conducted in India have revealed that teaching competence of student-teachers, who acquire teaching skills through micro-teaching approach, was higher than those who underwent experiences in learning to teach through traditional practice teaching programme.

The NCERT has developed an Indian model of micro-teaching on the basis of research studies conducted in this area. A number of colleges of education both at the elementary and secondary levels are using micro-teaching approach with a view to developing teaching skills among their student-teachers.

These skills are such as questioning, introducing the lesson, reinforcement, using audio-visual aids, writing instructional objectives, explaining, closure, diagnosing pupil's difficulties, etc.

Evaluate Yourself

1. Mention the main characteristics of learner-centred approach.
2. Mention four teaching strategies.
3. Teaching act can be analysed into a number of teaching skills. Write the names of five teaching skills which you consider are very important in teaching effectively in the classroom.

INCREASING USE OF ELECTRONIC GADGETS

Another trend in the teaching-learning process in our classroom is the use of electronic gadgets. A number schools have been provided computers under class project. A large number of schools in different states have been provided with television sets, radio-cum-cassette recorders, etc. Further, institutions, particularly public schools located in big towns have also procured white boards, e-podiluns. A greater use is therefore being made of audio and videoes in imparting instruction in the classroom.

In order to develop necessary skills among teachers to use hardwares and softwares appropriately, colleges of education—both the elementary and secondary levels—are being equipped with requisite hard and software. District Institutes of Education and Training have been equipped with computers, overhead projectors, white board videoes, etc. Similarly, Institutes of Advanced Studies in Education (IASEs) and CTEs are being strengthened in terms of these material resources.

RESURGENCE OF INTEREST IN ACTION RESEARCH

Action research is a form of research which addresses itself to the problems encountered by practitioners, i.e. teachers themselves in their work situation. The purpose by which practitioners attempt to study their problems scientifically in order to guide, correct and evaluate their decision and actions is what a number of people have called action research (Corey, 1953). The word 'action research' was coined by Kurt Lewin in 1944. Action research has been found to be an important means of teacher development.

Self-reflective spiral of cycles of planning, acting and observing is central to the action research approach. Kurt Lewin, who coined the phrase 'Action research' in 1944, described the process in terms of planning, fact finding and execution.

Stephen Corey, Kenneth Benne, Hilda Taba and Abraham Shumsky were early exponents of educational action research. After enjoying a decade of growth, action research went into decline in the late 1950s. The decline was attributable to the growing separation of research and action. The rising tide of post-sputnik curriculum development, based on a Research-Development-Diffusion (R, D and D) model of the relationship between research and practice, legitimated and sustained this separation.

The resurgence of interest in action research is again visible in the world. It is growing in Australia, in continental Europe and once again in the United States of America. There are a number of reasons for this. One of them is the demand from within an increasingly professionalized teaching force for a research role to investigate his/her own practice. Secondly, practitioners visualize that research findings do not have much relevance to their concerns. Thirdly, there is a greater awareness among practitioners that improvement in practices is possible through critical self-reflection.

As we may be knowing that action research is now a topic for study in teacher education curriculum of most of the universities, in-service teachers are also being encouraged to undertake action research to solve their problems.

TRANSACTION OF COMMON CORE COMPONENTS

The NPE (1986) envisaged that the National System of Education will be based on a national curricular framework which contains a common core along with other components that are flexible. The common core will include the history of India's freedom movement, the constitutional obligations and other content essential to nurture national identity. These elements will cut across subject areas and will be designed to promote values such as:

- History of India's freedom movement
- National Identity
- India's common cultural heritage
- egalitarianism
- democracy and socialism
- equality of sexes
- protection of the environment
- removal of social barriers
- observance of small family norms
- inculcation of the scientific temper

The teacher education curriculum may not include these core components as curricular areas, but the prospective teachers need to be familiarised with these components and equipped with suitable strategies to inculcate these values among their pupils.

MAINTENANCE OF STANDARDS OF TEACHERS EDUCATION

The National Council for Teacher Education (NCTE) was set up in 1973 by a government resolution as a national expert body to advise central and state government on all matters pertaining to teacher education. The NCTE's status and role have so far been purely advisory and mainly due to this reason, it has had very little impact on the standards of teacher education in the country and on their unplanned growth.

The National Policy on Education (1986) envisaged that the National Council for Teacher Education will be provided the necessary resources and capability to accredit institution of teacher education and to provide guidance regarding curricula and methods. The Programme of Action (POA) (1986) realising the inherent difficulties in the constitution of the NCTE to be able to guide the system of teacher education, envisaged conferring the NCTE with statutory status.

The central government is now introducing a bill in the parliament to confer the NCTE a statutory status. Once the NCTE becomes a statutory body, it will be its duty to take all such steps, as it may think fit for ensuring planned and co-ordinated development of teacher education and for the determination of standards of teacher education. The NCTE would lay down guidelines for compliance by recognised institutions for starting new course for providing physical and instructional facilities, staffing pattern, staff qualifications, etc. The council may, inter alia, cause inspection of any institution for the purpose of ascertaining whether the institutions are functioning in accordance with the provisions of the act.

Evaluate Yourself

1. Explain the reasons for resurgence of interest in action research.
2. Mention five common core components as envisaged in the National Policy on Education (1986).
3. Give the name of the body which will be responsible for maintenance of standards in teacher education.

FOUR YEAR INTEGRATED COURSE IN TEACHER EDUCATION

Another trend in teacher education is to have four year integrated course in teacher education for preparing secondary teachers. Four Regional Institutes of Education located at Ajmer, Bhopal, Bhubaneswar and Mysore are already in existence for the last so many years. These institutes are offering four year integrated course in teacher education. Minimum qualifications for admission to these colleges is 10+2. It is learnt that the University Grant Commission (UGC) panel on teacher education has recently recommended setting up more institutes of education in the country which may offer four year integrated course in teacher education. On completion of the course, students are awarded degrees i.e. B.A. B.Ed./B.Sc. B.com. B.Ed.

CENTRALISED ADMISSION TEST

It was highlighted in the document—Challenges of Education—A Policy Perspective, that in the case of teacher's training, the problem is not of equity of access but the relatively low standard of candidates. Considering the role assigned to education and the crucial position of teachers in it, it is necessary that admission to teacher's 'training institutions should be regulated through stringent aptitude and attainment tests'.

Now some state governments like Madhya Pradesh are making admission into their secondary colleges of education through admission tests. These tests generally include intelligence test, general knowledge test and aptitude test, etc.

SUMMARY

1. The objectives of school education are undergoing change as a result socio-economic, political changes, the stage of technological development of the society, etc.
2. The curriculum of school education also undergoes revision on account of changes in the objectives of school education.
3. Expanding horizons of knowledge, advances in pedagogical science, etc.
4. As a result of revision of school curriculum and its objectives, the programme of teacher education is also undergoing change.
5. There is a greater emphasis on practicum now.
6. Training of teachers in special education, changes in transaction approach, resurgence of interest in action research, increasing use of technology, emphasis on transaction of core component, etc. are some of the trends in teacher education programme.

MODEL ANSWERS

1. (i) (a) Internship in teaching including field assignments
   (b) Practical work including working with community, social work and work-experience
   (ii) Because practicum develops requisite skills among prospective teachers to discharge their responsibilities effectively as teacher.
   (iii) Yes, children with mild disabilities are also there in general classroom. Training of every teacher in special education is therefore, essential to deal with children.
   (iv) (a) Population Education
   (b) Women Education
   (c) Futurology in Education
   (d) Consumer Education
2. (i) (a) Stress in knowing the child
   (b) Emphasis on developing learning skill
   (c) Learning a joyful experience
   (d) Learning active participation
   (e) Learning through activities
   (ii) (a) Inquiry Training
   (b) Concept Attainment
   (c) Advance Organiser
   (d) Inductive Thinking
   (iii) (a) Skill of Explaining
   (b) Skill of Questioning
   (c) Skill of reinforcement
   (d) Skill of Illustrating with Examples
   (e) Skill of Stimulus Variation
3. (i) (a) Not much relevance of findings of research to the concerns of practitioners
   (b) Greater awareness among practitioners that improvement in practices is possible through critical self-reflection

(c) Teachers feel that they are capable of undertaking action research.

(ii) (a) Equality of sexes

(b) Observations of Small family norms

(c) Inculcation of Scientific temperament

(d) Protection of the social environment

(e) Removal of Social Barriers

KEYWORDS

Internship in Teaching. The term has been borrowed from medical education. In teacher education programme, a student teacher, after completing theory course and undergoing some preparatory experience, is sent as an intern to a school, where he works for a fixed period under the supervision of a school teacher.

Disabled Children. Disabled children refer to children with disabilities physical or mental.

Prospective Teacher. The term 'prospective teacher' stands for 'would be teachers'.

Transactional Approach. Transactional approach refers to the teaching approach which is used to teach in the classroom.

REFERENCES

Jangira, N.K. and Singh, Ajit (1984). *Core Teaching Skills—Microteaching*, New Delhi: NCERT.

MHRD (1986). National Policy on Education, New Delhi.

——— (1992). National Policy on Education (1986)—Programme of Action 1992, New Delhi.

Ministry of Education (1985). *Challenge of Education—A Policy Perspective*, New Delhi.

Passi, B.K. Singh, L.C. and Sansanwal, D.N. (1991). *Models of Teaching Report of Three Phase Study of CAM and ITM*, New Delhi: NCERT.

Singh, Ajit (1993). *Learner Centred Approach*, New Delhi (under print).

Singh, L.C. (Ed.) (1990). *Teacher Education in India—A Resource Book*, New Delhi: NCERT.

Singh, R.P. (1993). *The Challenges of Tomorrow—A Profile of Future Teacher Education*, New Delhi: Sterling Publishers Private Limited.

FURTHER READINGS

Saxena, N.R. Mishra, B.K. and Mohanty, R.K. (1998). *Teacher Education*, R. Lall Book Depot, Meerut (U.P.).

Sharma, R.A. (2002). *Teacher Education*; International Publication House, Meerut, U.P.

Shukla, R.S. (1978). *Emerging Trends in Teacher—Education*, Chugh Publications, Allahabad.

Soward (1980). Model of Teacher Education (in R.A. Sharma: Teacher Education, International Publication House, Meerut (U.P.).

Srivastava, R.C. and Bose, K. (1973). *Theory and Practice of Teacher Education in India*, Chugh Publications, Allahabad.

Storm, R.D. (1971). *Teaching and Learning Process*, Prentice Hall Inc. Englewood Cliffs, New Jersey.

Tibble, J.W. (1971). *Future of Teacher Education*, Routledge and Kegan Paul, London.

UNESCO Publication (1977). Exploring New Dimensions in Teacher Education, Bangkok Report.

Chapter 8

Teacher Education Programme in U.K.

STRUCTURE OF CHAPTER

- Introduction
- Teacher Education Programme in U.K.
  - Present System of Education
  - Development of Teacher Education
  - Present Teacher Education System
  - Induction and In-service Training
- Summary
- Evaluate Yourself
- Model Answers
- Keywords
- References
- Further Readings

INTRODUCTION

This chapter is an attempt to develop understanding of the teacher education programme in U.K. by drawing parallels with the Indian system of teacher. In chapter two, teacher education programme with special reference to present teacher education system and in-service training of teachers have been discussed.

TEACHER EDUCATION PROGRAMME IN U.K.

The quality of the teacher education programme, both at pre-service and in-service level, determines the quality of teaching in schools. The initial inputs with regards to the potential of the entrants into the profession interact with the subsequent ones, at the pre-service stage and with consecutive exposure too. Only when teaching is accepted as a profession will teacher education be considered a professional course. The importance a country gives to its education system is reflected in the concern for preparing its teachers.

Present System of Education

In Britain today, there is compulsory education from 6 to 16 years of age.

The Local Education Authorities (LEAs) manage and administer education for children within their jurisdiction. They run primary and secondary schools and even award scholarships. The only schools at secondary level where there is selection are the comprehensive schools run by the LEA. The others at this level are technical, secondary and grammar schools as also the expressive public schools from where entry to the university is fairly smooth examinations are of the normal variety as also to give scholarships.

Since the status of teacher training is low as in the US, India and elsewhere, good students do not go in for teacher training. Therefore, the grammar and public schools do not insist on training for their teachers, which is a practice in many primate schools and the KVS (Kendriya Vidyalaya Schools) at +2 stage in India also.

Its Background: It was only in the late 19th and the first quarter of the 20th century that the relevance of school education received the attention of the Parliament. In 1926, secondary education was accepted as the preparation to university; subsequently, primary stage was accepted as the earlier link in the chain. However, it is noteworthy that the British Parliament in 1870, acknowledged the government's responsibility in providing elementary education to the entire population in the age group. Here in India as well, the British attitude was clearly reflected in their setting up of universities in the Presidency towns rather than catering to the common man.

Development of Teacher Education

Orientation for teaching is unfortunately associated with a low status and still carries it along. The early form of teacher preparation was the monitorial system evolving as a need to cope with the increasing numbers in schools. The system necessitated teaching the older ones in school so that they could be assigned the responsibility of teaching their younger ones. A strategy to cope with large groups was Stow's 'simultaneous system'. Between 1836-46, several training colleges were established by a society. Shuttleworth, in 1840, established a foundation which introduced very significant development 2; good students in the elementary were offered the chance to stay on and become apprenticed to an experienced teacher at the age of 13. Thus continued his own studies as well as learning skills of 'handling' children.

The period of apprenticeship continued till 18+, in some cases lasting almost five years, followed by a centrally conducted examination by the Education Department on the completion of which a certificate for reaching was awarded and which was introduced nationally by the Committee of the Privy Council.

Seeing this support, colleges began to look to the government—scholarships and grant to institutions began to be awarded. The Department of Science and Education began to provide curricular, hold examinations and award certificates. Subsequently, the standards of trainees declined. To overcome the problem, early academic training (teaching the subject content) was also passed on to the colleges who introduced context-cum-methodology courses in several colleges and university departments of education of Indian Universities and also in the RIEs, till the recent past. And after 1902, this was taken up by grammar schools for secondary education.

The Educational Department prepared regulations for grant-aided day colleges along with universities. The colleges offered the three years courses wherein academic and professional studies ran concurrently for a university degree, along with a certificate—a situation wherein the university is the examining body. By the beginning of this century the academic degree was of three years duration followed by a one year's professional certificate thus, the three year colleges became four year education colleges—the prevailing pattern in U.K. where in these colleges grew into University Departments of Education and in India the B.Ed. formula. This pattern became very popular particularly with different religious bodies providing residential courses. In 1902, LEAs were created by the Education Act of 1902 who established similar but better day 'municipal' training colleges, mainly because of the inherent differences.

This act brought to an end the pupil tender system and the four years of secondary education enabled entry into these colleges. The Burham Committee of Enquiry made recommendations whereby the system of education, which was the Board of Education's responsibility, be transferred to the board of university and colleges, the former becoming the examining body.

The colleges were reorganised into regional groups, each under a university which formulated curricula, organised the external examination while the Board of Education held the right to examine the efficiency of the practical training.

The Nair Commission redefined secondary education from 14 upto 15½, for the General Certificate of Education. A number of teachers' colleges were temporarily set up for providing a 13-month intensive training; some of the colleges continued.

The Robbens Committee in 1963 suggested that enrolment in colleges should be increased; the opportunity to obtain a university degree with a professional one—the four year course at which Bachelor of Education (B.Ed.) be awarded total years of University education equivalent to open in India.

In 1972, the report titled "Teacher Education and Training" (by Lord James) suggested reform and reorganisation of teacher education. The government and concerned bodies came together and the National Advisory Council for Training and Supply of Teachers (NACTST) was replaced by the Advisory Committee on Supply Council for Training (ACSCT). Besides 'induction' programmes for new teacher in-service training, a graduate teaching profession, and replacement of university-based Area Training Organisation (ATOs) by new regional committees was undertaken; the status of the university departments of education was very low.

Present Teacher Education System

The National Council for Teacher Education and Training and its fifteen regional committees are now coordinating the department of education and the training colleges. The LEAs have also been reorganised and not all have retained the responsibility of education. Fall in birth rates and unemployment among teachers have been considered while implementing the James Committee Report (1972) and colleges were merged or closed down.

- Two Years Diploma in higher education is offered by the colleges of education to those who continue in the third year of B.Ed. degree and after the fourth year a B.Ed. (Hons) degree. Most offer the four-year course.

  The colleges of education are either (i) independent, (ii) located in a Liberal Arts College, (iii) as a department of a polytechnic, or (iv) in a college of further education. They are either for men, women, or co-educational.

  The curriculum over the three year period has varying emphasis comparing lectures 5-6 times a week as a general introduction to education with reference to child psychology and development, general methods and on issues along with lecturers and discussion, three hours a week on a main subject not necessarily an academic subject, two subsidiary subjects, 1-2 hrs. per week, content cum methodology of common subjects like physical education and religious knowledge, English and the like four hrs. a week; at the onset a week of observation and later three weeks of practice teaching.

  In the second year, the professional studies, the main subject and subsidiary subjects continue and this time, four weeks of practice teaching indicates a trend towards specialisation.

  In the third year, the professional studies continue taking up more time and with greater emphasis on general study and specialisation in an area, continuation of the main subject, practice teaching of 7-8 weeks as well as study of a special paper for the final comprehensive examination.

- The Council of National Academic Awards (CNAA), parallel to the university system, validates the college degrees. This provides an institution considerable autonomy with flexibility for frequently changing without the problems of conformity to the rigid norms of the university system.
- **The University Department of Education** now awards a post-graduate certificate in education (PGCE) after a student has completed the B.A. or B.Sc. degree. This was earlier awarded by the ATOs, but several colleges of education are also awarding the B.Ed. degree.
- **Admission Procedures:** University Department of Education, Colleges of Education and Polytechnics prepare teachers and offer each of the three level courses which are B.Ed. (Hons.) after four years, B.Ed. after three years and Diploma in Higher Education, after two years.

  Those enrolling in polytechnics or colleges of education generally have a GCE with one or two A level courses, not very many have two. The minimum, requirement is five subjects at 'O' level but in some cases there are more 'A' level courses and the number of 'O' level may be lesser.
- **Alternate Facilities:** College have provision for students who are unable to attend the regular ones.
- Short-term courses are arranged for those who were students earlier and subsequently seek entry into teaching. Part-time courses are offered for married women by many colleges and a few university departments.

  In Home Economics Colleges, a B.Ed. degree with emphasis on home economics, domestic science along with sciences and social sciences is offered; the home science component includes home making, child rearing, and the like.

Besides the teacher training in physical education provided by physical education colleges is also offered by many other colleges.

Colleges of technical education, of which there are just a handful, prepare teachers for further education as well as technical colleges through the several courses available for specialist teachers. The initial training of these further colleges is also being stressed upon, a one year's pre-service training exists for those interested in preparing themselves before taking up a job. This is organised like the PGCE, training while working (in-service training is available, spread over four terms. Besides, part time courses are also available at centres where individual come to study technical suggests as a basis for understanding other related things.

Those already trained in art can obtain a professional training in art through teacher training centres at polytechnics. These receive the official approval of the Department of Education and Science.

University departments of education and colleges of education offer a one year course to graduates leading to a post graduate certificate in education. The ten to thirteen weeks of block practice teaching accompany the professional studies occurring anywhere in the year. This is very similar to a B.Ed. in India.

- The Bachelor of Education Degree (B.Ed.) has several forms varied, but in essence, it is either a three or four years course, depending on the type offered. The colleges of education affiliated to universities offer the four year B.Ed. (B.Ed. Hons.), insisting on higher entry qualifications while where the CNAA validates, each of the three types are offered: (i) a diploma in Higher education, two-year after GCE with one or two 'A' level courses; (ii) B.Ed. in three years; and (iii) B.Ed. (Hons.) in four years like in the colleges of education affiliated to Universities.

The B.Ed. in these consists of 15 weeks of practice teaching.

Induction and In-service Training

A certificate or degree in teaching is necessarily followed by a year on the job. This year is a probation period and supervised. The school is selected by the Local Education Authority (LEA) or the Department of Education and Science. Performance in this probation period determines the individual's entry or induction into teaching it. Only on successful completion of the induction programme is a prospective teacher licensed to teach; a registration number is awarded just like in medicine. The introduction of this induction was as per the recommendation of the James Report (1972).

With the assumption that an individual involved with teaching requires continuous supervision and support, the James report also recommended in-service training every seven years; in India, it is envisaged every five years. This in-service training is envisaged as an opportunity to acquire higher qualifications by which upward mobility to colleges and inspectorate is possible. Institutions offering these courses are University Departments of Education, Colleges of Education and their counterparts as well the Council of National Academic Awards (CNAA). They offer programmes of varying duration. The graduate degree for all teachers in schools is the goal along with regular training facilities. Alongside, 550 teachers' centres for keeping abreast with curriculum development have been set up.

For those teachers who are neither graduates nor trained, the open University of the U.K. offers a special programme a B.A. in Educational Studies. Those possessing a three-years teacher's certificate, need to complete three credits rather than six and for a B.A. Honours degree five credits instead of eight.

The open university offers a considerably wide opportunity, and a course on educational technology for classrooms particularly for teachers.

SUMMARY

1. Teacher education in the U.K. is undergoing a period of change with the emergence of new courses.

2. The Council of National Academic Awards is filling in the gap left by the universities.
3. All higher and further education outside the universities, including teacher education is being assimilated into a common system under the control of local education authorities.
4. However, the superiority of the universities remains, salaries are on the basis of qualifications and on the not level or stage of taught, however, at the lower level, the teachers have less qualifications as teaching is not a popular choice of good students just as in India.
5. Then, the institutions closest to the administrative centres or larger towns are the ones more sought after and also more effective.
6. Unlike India, the government looks to the quality, number and positioning of the teachers and pays the unemployment ones as this number has increased with the reduction of positions and institutions and because of decrease in birth rates and general policy of reducing expenditures. For instance, by doing away with special schools and opting for main-streaming or integration of disabled children.
7. The professional growth of practising teachers is a responsibility taken up by local authorities universities and colleges like the state governments are doing for the teachers in government schools in Indian through the SCERTS, DIETS and as in IASEs established as a result of NPE, 1986 and revised policy (1992).

Evaluate Yourself

In tabular form, compare the teacher training facilities in U.K. to that of in India under the heads (i) Pre-service (ii) In-service.

MODEL ANSWERS

Please, consult section.

KEYWORDS

Monitorial System. The system of teaching the elder ones in school so that they could be assigned the responsibility of teaching their younger ones.

Home Economics College. A college offering B.Ed. degree with emphasis on home economics and domestic science along with science and social sciences.

REFERENCES

Bhattacharya, G. (1990). *Teacher Education*, Vinod Pustak Mandir, Arga (U.P.).

Combs, A.W. (1964). The Personal Approach to Good Teaching, Educational Leadership.

Deway, J. (1916). *Democracy and Education*, MacMillan Book Co., New York.

Gage, N.L. (1963). "The Theories of Teaching" (in N.L. Gago (Ed.): *Handbook of Research on Teaching*, McNally & Co., Chicago.

Gupta, A.K. (1988). *Teacher Education*, Sterling Publishers, New Delhi.

Khan, M.S. (1983). *Teacher Education in India and Abroad*, New Delhi, Ashish Publishing House.

Korner, James D. (1968). *Reforms in Education*, London, Weldenfeld Necolson.

FURTHER READINGS

Buch, M.B. (Ed. 1974). *Survey of Research in Education*, Centre of Advanced study in Education, M.S. University of Baroda, Vadodara.

Challenges of Education Policy Perspectives (1985). Ministry of Human Resource Development, Govt. of India, New Delhi.

Mehta, C.S. and Joshi, D.C. (1973). *Principles and Problems of Teacher Education* Part I & II (in Hindi), Rajasthan Hindi Granth Academy, Jaipur.

Morrison, A. and McIntyre, D. (1969). *Teacher and Teaching*, Armonds Worth, Penguin.

Report (1986). Programme of Action: New Education Policy, MHRD Govt. of India, New Delhi.

Saxena, N.R. Mishra, B.K. and Mohanty R.K. (1998). *Teacher Education*, R. Lall Book Depot, Meerut (U.P.).

Sharma, R.A. (2002). *Teacher Education*, International Publishing House, Meerut (U.P.).

Shukla, R.S. (1978). *Emerging Trends in Teacher Education*, Chug Publications, Allahabad.

Smith, B.O. (1971). *Research in Teacher Education: A Symposium*, Prentice Hall Inc. Englewood Cliff, New Jersey.

Stones, E. and Morris, S. (1972). *Teaching Practice: Problems and Perspectives*, Methuen and Co. Ltd., London.

Tibble, J.W. (1971). *Future of Teacher Education*, Routledge and Kegan Paul, London.

Chapter 9

Teacher Education Programme in U.S.A.

STRUCTURE OF CHAPTER

- Introduction
- Structure of Education
- Development of Teacher Education
  - Teacher Training: Agencies, Levels and Course Inputs
  - Maintaining Standards
  - Levels of Teacher Preparation
  - National Education Association
  - Curriculum for Elementary Teaching
- National Commission on Excellence in Education
- Summary
- Evaluate Yourself
- Key Words
- References
- Further Readings

INTRODUCTION

Though the USA is presently the most powerful nation economically, among the most affluent, and the rest of the world greatly affected by its policies, and hence trying to often keep in step with their policies, the administration continually strives to see that it remains a forerunner in the field of education also. This effort is despite the fact that education is basically a state subject. However, the federal government, like our Central Government, does contribute to educational effort. In the USA, this amount is approximately three per cent and most if it goes into support research as well as education of the poor—mainly immigrants and Afro-Americans. It is in this context that considerable research effort is undertaken on other countries and their systems so as to understand them as well as to remain ahead. The state departments of education are in a way similar to India's as the political decisions tend to influence educational decisions. However, with regards to implementation and management of the rest of the educational system, the community's representatives run it. Thus, educational administration is run by a combination of laymen and experts with frequent shifts in the power block.

STRUCTURE OF EDUCATION

High school education is free, covering all other related expenditure and compulsory between the ages of 6 to 16 in most states. The few private ones are experimental ones however university and college education is entirely fee paying unlike India and therefore, rather expensive.

Some adult education centres do exist, but they are different from ours. They run on demand programmes for social problems including adjustment of certain groups as well as organise training/updating in advanced skills; their clientele is however, not very large.

Universities are mainly state-run, with a campus over the entire state; other are privately run. The names are derived on the basis of management.

Structure of education and schooling in the U.S. is of 12 years duration, like in India with a 8+4 break up; preschool education is accepted by all. In fact, the importance of early experiences has been greatly emphasised subsequent to federal level research effort to evaluate its lasting impact, with the intention of having the most creative scientists in the world.

There are a variety of institutions and liberal arts colleges, where the first degree (graduation in India) takes three years, while professional courses with a degree are of four or more years. These are purely professional colleges and the most common type of institutions are called community colleges wherein a wide variety of courses, of varying duration, are available. Classes are held right through the day to enable anyone who can pay to join.

Each institution conducts its own examination and gives a degree, both at school and college level. At school level, there are variations in textbooks and teaching however, this lack of 'homogeneity'—as in India—does not pose barriers to mobility. This is probably because of the social mobility of the people. Anyone interested in getting certified as an effective teacher, may get tested by the Educational Testing service on an external examination.

DEVELOPMENT OF TEACHER EDUCATION

In the U.S. like elsewhere, teacher education began on experimentation basis—initially as a private enterprise, to try out the models adopted in France and Prussia, as early at 1785. In 1820, Samuel Hall established an experimental training school to try out the theory or model he had propounded in his writings. The first public teacher training institution was established in 1839. Until then, all efforts at teacher training were focused on the elementary school through a 2-year course. It was sometime later that training programmes for secondary education were conceived.

By 1870, separate colleges for elementary and teacher training emerged and simultaneously some universities also began to become interested in teacher training and set up 'chairs' or earmarked positions for pedagogy. During, this, the two-year courses at normal schools were converted into four-year teacher education institutions and simultaneously, universities began setting up departments of education with the school attached with them. Thus, these independent institutions—university departments of education and teacher colleges—started setting new trends and improved teacher education in the U.S.A.

Teacher Training: Agencies Levels and Course Inputs

Initially, normal schools prepared the elementary teachers and the teachers colleges and universities prepared both elementary and secondary level teachers. By the 60's, the teachers colleges were converted into multipurpose institutions in the form of comprehensive colleges and universities and offered a variety of specialisation in different areas of education—first-degree, masters degree and doctoral level programmes, and teacher training. There are institutions in India as well that are acting as comprehensive colleges—if not completely at least partially. In fact, in the POA (1986) and the revised POA (1992), such institutions have been envisaged.

These comprehensive colleges prepare teachers to teach all classes at each level of school education namely, pre-primary, elementary and high school, for different school subjects. Several universities' department of education are now offering courses of different specialisation at masters and Master of Philosophy (M.Phil.) levels besides preparing teachers for various tasks at different levels of school education.

Teachers for schools in America, are mainly prepared in university departments of education, some of these courses are offered at the graduate level while others provide the training at graduate and undergraduate levels.

The structure of education includes colleges offering courses for 3 and 4 years. Most four year colleges offer teacher training courses with the aforementioned (university departments) as well as several other types of institutions. The four year colleges may be divided into four categories.

(1) The liberal arts colleges offer no vocational course other than teacher training;

(2) Private colleges have now introduced teacher training as one of the vocational courses/programmes;

(3) The state colleges like the private colleges, are offering vocational courses, including teacher training; and

(4) The last category, state colleges in which over 3/4ths of those enrolled plan to become teachers. Hence, it is only the last mentioned category that is basically a teacher training institute.

In India, these are named as the teacher training colleges, either government/state run or private, offering the 1-year teacher training (B.Ed.) at graduate level to prepare teachers for upper primary and high school classes (classes VI to X).

Within this course, some of them have provisions for taking in the postgraduate in a subject and train them to teach senior secondary classes (classes XI and XII). A department of education in the privately run liberal arts colleges in some parts of northern India, also runs such course Primary teachers are prepared in elementary teacher training institutions, both privately and government (state) run, since NPE (1986) and POA (1992) District Institutions of Education (DIETS one in each district, run by the state government).

The number of teacher training institutions which serve only the training purpose are very few and gradually declining.

Every teacher training course has essentially three components: general education, specialisation in field of interest and professional education. The 4-year integrated courses at the Regional Institute of Education (RIEs) in India, offer such courses while the others offer foundation courses (philosophy, sociology and psychology) with professional education in two school subjects, (the course includes student teaching and internship).

Maintaining Standards

The emphasis on maintaining standards in education including teacher education is a factor contributing to the well being of the American system. The control on standards is through the processes of accreditation and certification. A specialised agency recognises and approves the institutions, its programmes and facilities, on the basis of specified standards, and gives approval to individuals to teach. This approval to the institutions and subsequently their students to teach as per their training, is done at the local, state, regional and national level. Earlier (towards the end of the 19th century), a school committee which was not necessarily competent to do so, gave local certificates. These certificates licensed those who had attended a teacher training course to teach accordingly. The State Department of Education took on this responsibility.

By 1946, the National Education Association (NEA) set up a National Commission on teachers education along with evolving of professional standards. This was incorporated in a document manual titled "Manual on Certification Requirement for School Personnel U.S." and suggested its revision once in three years so as to cater for emerging needs and focuses of status as well as the nation.

National Commission recommended a bachelor's degree as the minimum level for preparation to train as a teacher; all schools were advised to follow in order to receive state and national accreditation.

A variety of certificates are indicated in the manual and can be categorised on the basis of level of preparation, teaching position or assignment, and duration of validity.

Levels of Teacher Preparation

The level of teacher preparation for which certification are provided are varied in order to meet emergent requirements. This variety is probably based on the assumption that some orientation in teaching, irrespective of calibre, is better than no orientation. Certification of a teacher to handle tasks at hand is quite heterogenous so that the school can hire a teacher to handle specific tasks/activities of the school curriculum either general or limited to a specific area or subject. On the certificate of a specialised teacher, each authorised teaching area, field or subject has been indicated. Teachers who have specialised in a specific field get a separate certificate for each, or the special field is indicated on the authorisation or certificate.

Teachers trained for pre-school and primary (elementary) schools receive a general certificate while those trained to teach upper primary and secondary level (B.Ed.) have their two specialised teaching subjects indicated on it. Sometimes they receive mark sheets with their competency to handle their activities like community work, SUPW and the like mentioned thereon. Some institutions/universities give separate certificate for each of the activities for which the student-teacher's skills have been sharpened. The duration for which the certificate is awarded is probably a result of a combination of factors like length of training, mode of training (extent of contact and practice) and performance level or competencies developed in the teacher.

Full certification takes five years of teacher preparation, the last year of which has to be completed within specified period after the initial four year certification. Most of these teachers are graduates, like in our four year integrated course, while the administrative and supervisory staff must possess a masters degree in most states or atleast six years of higher education in some others. The National Teacher Examination certification to teachers throughout the country is the most widely used examination.

Since the certificates are of varying levels, there is provision for up gradation of competencies and renewal of certificate for teachers in service through in-service courses.

By holding the reins, the NEA is able to determine, maintain and raise standards (of the teacher training institutions and ultimately the teachers) by the stringent periodical, evaluation of the infrastructure resources and inputs against their standards and norms. The Regional Associations of Colleges were set up to establish standards in education and also to provide guidelines to the institutions. The American Association of Teachers (Colleges) was developed and began accrediting its members. It was later known as American Association of Teacher Education, assumed responsibility for evaluating and accrediting the concerned institutions and providing standards for different levels of accreditation national, regional and the like.

In India, the National Council of Teacher Education (NCTE) is in the way of being given these powers, once the bill is passed in the parliament.

The National Education Association (NEA)

NEA works to raise the status and further interests of the teaching profession and basic education in the U.S. being the largest professional organisation in the world encompassing all teachers and all aspects of education there. It has a hierarchical structure comprising departments, headquarter divisions and several commissions and committees, to facilitate its objectives among which prominently figure: (i) high quality instruction, (ii) adequate facilities and materials, (iii) favourable teaching conditions, (iv) teacher welfare, (v) protection of rights of teachers, (vi) professional standards, and (vii) active public support to education.

To work towards achieving these, the NEA conducts research, publishes journals for dissemination and sharing of ideas and experiences and problems as well as a monthly Reporter (newsletter) besides utilising mass media, field services and professional Negotiations and welfare services for the members. It is also undertaking projects for in house functioning and development as well as affiliated associations at state and local level.

The improved quality of school education and teacher education today has been achieved by the NEA. Its National Commission on Teachers' Education and Professional Standards evolved the National Council for Accreditation of Teacher Education to achieve its objectives at the grass root level. It is hoped that a regulatory set up will emerge in India too, once the NCTE attains statutory status.

Curriculum for Elementary Teaching

The duration of preparation varies from two to four years, while for teaching at the secondary stage it is four years and in a few states it is five years. The fifth year is essential for certification (discussed earlier). At the end of the integrated 4-year course, a bachelors' degree is awarded, wherein the foundation level courses in education are offered along with professional understanding. The autonomy to institutions and within a state has led to the development of merely two curriculum organisations:

(i) General education in first two years and next two years to professional development.

(ii) General education and professional development are developed simultaneously.

The four year integrated course at the Regional Institute of Education and Kurukshetra University were developed on these models. For instance, in the RIE at Mysore, Ajmer and Bhopal, the first year is purely general education with foundations in education introduced in the second year and more emphasis to the specialization of discipline in the third year. Some other foundation level courses are offered along with professional course and observation and teaching in school with a slight increase in weightage and time to the basic discipline (maths, science: language, social science). In the final year, the fourth year, professional input remains along with further development of understanding. No general education courses are offered in the last two years. In RIE Bhubaneshwar students could opt for a bachelors degree in the discipline after completing three years, wherein the foundations in education were offered. Those who continued for the fourth year were awarded the integrated degree B.Sc. Ed. or B.A. Ed.

In the better teacher training institutions and university departments having teacher training, considerable weightage and time is devoted to the organisation and involvement in curricular activities. The teacher education curricula for various levels of school education developed by the NCTE lay, emphasis on the same.

As mentioned earlier, on the successful completion of teacher training, the certification to practice or license to teach is awarded either by the state department of education or by the state certificate board and later by the national body. On the basis of this a teaching assignment is sought. Also, the need for the fifth year (of work in school) input for certification is becoming more and more popular with the employers.

Teacher training for pre-school stage (diploma in nursery or pre-school education) is being desired by the employers.

Jobs are applied directly to the local school board (the major employer) or through a placement service. Appointments are contractual (for a certain time period); regulations safeguarding service, retirement and sickness benefits and the like vary from state to state.

National Commission on Excellence in Education

Set up in 1981, the Commission submitted its report titled "A Nation At Risk" in 1983. The Commission was appointed to look into the problems afflicting teacher education encompassing teachers' strike incompetency and callousness of teachers indiscipline in schools. These problems had their roots elsewhere—shortage of competent (content-wise) teachers in mathematics, science, computer science and other emerging areas as well as in English language and literature.

Good students seek other professions because of the low status in society, low salaries and poor service conditions of teachers.

The American Federation of Teachers suggests a testing of teachers before they are hired just as state governments and local bodies are beginning to adopt in India.

The National Commission on Excellence in Education (NCEE) has recommended:

(i) Selective admission to teacher training programmes on the basis of subject competency.

(ii) Increase in salaries.

(iii) Minimum of 11-months teacher contracts to enable planning and implementation of complete programmes for children with special needs, curriculum and professional development.

(iv) Development of hierarchical set up among teachers on the basis of beginning instructors, experienced teachers and master teachers with the help of school boards, administrators and the teachers.

(v) Outside personal can be brought into the school to meet immediate shortage of competent teachers. Leading subject centres, resources may be utilised to update teachers.

(vi) Offering of incentives, loans, grants to outstanding students to attract to teaching profession.

(vii) Master teachers (in India known as resource persons) involvement in designing teacher preparation programmes and supervising teachers on probation (in India, they also supervise practice teaching and internship of student trainees)

Evaluate Yourself

Schematically (in the form of a figure) present the U.S. school structure and the prevailing teacher training for it.

SUMMARY

1. High school education in USA is free and compulsory between the age 6 to 16 years. Schooling in the U.S. is of 12 years duration like in India, with a 8 + 4 breakup.
2. Beyond high school level, there are a variety of institutions such as liberal arts colleges, purely professional colleges and community colleges.
3. Each institution conducts its own examination and gives degree both at school and college level.
4. The first teacher training institute was established in 1839.
5. Initially normal schools prepared elementary teachers and the teacher's colleges and universities prepared elementary and secondary level teachers.
6. The control of standard in education is through the process of accreditation and certification.
7. A specialized agency recognises and approves the institutions. Its programmes and facilities are on the basis of specified standards and gives approval to individuals to teach.
8. Teachers trained for pre-school and primary (elementary) schools receive general certificate while those trained to teach the upper primary and secondary level have their two specialized teaching subjects indicated on it.
9. The National Teacher Examination, which issues certificates to teach throughout the country is the most widely used examination.
10. The status and quality of education is continuously reviewed by an agency known as National Education Association (NEA).

11. It works for high quality instructions and facilities at school level, jobs are applied directly to the local school board (the major employer) or to it through placement service.

KEYWORDS

Liberal Arts Colleges. Colleges offering three years degree course called first degree, comparable to graduation in India.

Community Colleges. Colleges offering a wide variety of courses of varying durations.

Comprehensive Colleges. Colleges which prepare teachers to teach all classes at each level of school education, namely pre-primary, elementary and high school teachers.

REFERENCES

Khan, M.S. (1983). *Teacher Education in India and Abroad*, New Delhi: Ashish Publication House.

Kooner, James D. (1968). *Reforms in Education*, London, Weildfield Nicolson.

Saxena, N.R., Mishra, B.K. and Mohanty, R.K. (1998). *Teacher Education*, R. Lall Book Depot, Meerut.

Sharma, R.A. (2002). *Teacher Education*, International Publishing House, Meerut (U.P.).

Shukla, R.S. (1978). *Emerging Trends in Teacher Education*, Chugh Publications, Allahabad.

FURTHER READINGS

Bhattacharya, G.S. (1990). *Teacher Education*, Vinod Pustak Mandir, Agra (U.P.).

Gupta, A.K. (1988). *Teacher Education*, Sterling Publishers, New Delhi.

Herbart, J.F. (1904). *Outlines of Educational Doctrine*. MacMillan Book Co., New Delhi.

Hough, J.B. and Duncan, J.K. (1970). *Teaching: Description and Analysis*, Addison Wesley, California.

Sharma, R.A. (1980). *Technology of Teaching: Teacher Behaviour*, Loyal Book Depot, Meerut.

Shukla, R.S. (1989). *Shiksha Shiksha: Disha Evam Disha* (in Hindi) Akshat Prakashan, Udaipur, Rajasthan.

Teacher Education Curriculum A Framework (1996). NCTE—Publication, New Delhi.

UNESCO Publication (1977). Exploring New Delhi Dimensions in Teacher Education Bangkok (Report).

——— (1978). Continuing Education for Teacher Educators, Bangkok (Report).

Chapter 10

Teacher Education Programme in Russia

STRUCTURE OF CHAPTER

- Introduction
- Structure of Education
- Teacher Training
  - Teacher Training Schools
  - Pedagogical Institute
  - Correspondence Pedagogical Institute
  - Academy of Pedagogical Science
  - In-service Education Programmes
- Changing Trends
- Evaluate Yourself
- Summary
- Model Answers
- Keywords
- References
- Further Readings
- Learning Exercise

INTRODUCTION

The political and economic settings have a direct bearing on the education system that prevails in the nation. In the erstwhile Russia, this was all the more as the communist manifesto had so much to say on the role of education as well as on the type of education that should prevail. The communist manifesto called for free education for the children and the possibility of being involved in economic activity while pursuing education.

With the recent breakup of the Union of Soviet Socialist Republic and establishment of an independent state, the prevailing education system has not undergone any change, that is the structure and practices that existed at the time of the break up, continue to exist.

It is in this light that the underlying assumptions and emphasis of the Soviet model, a specific kind of education is needed to liberate society from age-old attitudes and ways of responding which are no longer appropriate and acceptable. Since language is a vehicle of communication and hence provides access to knowledge and its study is imperative; repetitive strategies restrain an individual from acquiring meaningful experience. Therefore, technical knowledge wherein the entire cycle (of production) of activity is viewed in a gestalt, hence enabling the development of positive attitudes towards the common group and individuals therein.

Education was viewed as the chief instrument for establishing and maintaining social order, therefore attendance was made compulsory and free. To enable schooling and work to develop simultaneously, productive work was incorporated in the school programme to enable mental and physical skills to integrate. A common programme of instruction was adopted so as to provide common background training to all with the intent of developing a feeling that each one has a useful role to play.

Since the development of man figured in the manifesto; young children were not the mother's sole responsibility by providing facilities for physical and mental development. Thus, emerged an educational programme 'from the cradle to the grave.' It would be worthwhile to know their school system to understand the teacher education programme/s.

STRUCTURE OF EDUCATION

We need to study the structure/stages at the school level, the curriculum, optionals, vocational subjects and extramural activities together to understand a country's school education. The institution like the Indian formal system reveal the various emphasis as is listed:

(a) **Pre School Set Up** is the first step in providing for the child's upbringing and care up to six years. The alternatives are creches, kindergartens creches and other pre- schools establishments thus freeing the family from caring for the child and enabling the human resource to participate. For convenience, this age group is divided into early (including 1, 2 and 3 year olds) and senior (4, 5 and 6 year olds) groups.

The institution for this age group brings up the child together with the family so that family may even be expected to spend time at the institution. The concerns are health immunisation and nutrition (medical help), independence training (self-help and cooperation), develop aesthetic sense and prepare them for primary school by developing fundamental skills to learn writing, speaking, ability to observe, classify, categorise and the like. A doctor is attached and necessary medical care is also organised for.

The number of children going to primary/elementary school after kindergarten is growing. This stage is looked at preparation for later schooling. The process of this preparation or methods and strategies has been identified on the basis of research, as what is adopted in the U.S., and under progressive system in India that is interaction with presents and other adults, experiences to develop sound and visual discrimination.

(b) **General Secondary Education:** School education is universal and compulsory for a period of 11 years and comprises four years of primary school (forms 1 to 4) and five years of a complete secondary education (forms 5 to 9). The non-Russian language and evening schools may even be of longer duration. Six year olds enter the extended primary school.

Primary education attempts to provide elementary knowledge in eight subjects comprising drawing, singing, native language, physical training, reading, mathematics, natural science and labour training, and also Russian in the national schools. The primary stage is viewed as a foundation for secondary and senior forms.

Upto form 8 (primary-4 and incomplete secondary education till form 8) is the schooling all have to attend: form 8 is a terminal stage (upper primary in India).

(c) **Through Curriculum Content and treatment** in syllabus and textbooks exposure to polytechnic training begins here itself through labour training and by incorporating branches of production, trades, economics and organisation of production, variety of enterprises and the like. In India curriculum also the compulsory 10 years of schooling include some elements of there and it is much more so at +2 stage.

(d) **After form eight** (the common schooling for all) pupils are awarded a certificate for:

(i) Form 9 of general school, at the end of which secondary education certificate is awarded to enable entry into specialised secondary schools, vocational schools or higher secondary schools.

(ii) Specialised secondary school.

(iii) Vocational schools.

(e) **In the common schooling,** twenty subjects are taught—native language, literature, history, social science, economics, physical geography, physics, chemistry, biology (including botany, zoology, anatomy, physiology and hygiene), astronomy, algebra, geometry, trigonometry, music, art, physical training, labour training and draughtsmanship opportunity for taking up optional subjects is available from seven, with the intent of providing a wider general, basic, greater opportunity to develop the learner's internals and abilities through the knowledge developed by further study.

Some exposure to polytechnic training commences in general secondary schools like branches of production, leading trades, economics and organisation of labour. In specailized secondary schools, the certification at the end of form eight is on the basis of performance and aptitudes for which testing is done. It is an extensive opportunity to develop interests and aptitudes provided through the variety of facilities available.

Specialised secondary schools are intended to provide deeper knowledge into subjects like art, mathematics, physics, chemistry, biology or foreign language. Entry into art, mathematics or physics and mathematics schools is on a very competitive basis, intended only for the gifted.

Optional course work in a specific subject may be taken up with a definite maximum time limit.

(f) **Vocational Secondary Schools:** Presently, more than half of the students go in for general secondary education (grade 9) and then terminate their education. The remaining go in for some form of specialization.

The rudiments of vocationalisation (handling of equipment and tools) are introduced in the first eight forms of general secondary education, therefore subsequently, selection is on the basis of interest development through the previous exposure.

They begin visiting training and production centres in form 7 as part of labour training.

(g) **Facilities for Extramural Activities:** The Ministry of Education has a very wide network of institutions which enables children in schools to participate and develop. Two hours per week in the schools is considered adequate.

These extramural institutions organise sports groups within a neighbourhood to enable them to play after school. Through the network, competitions are possible all over the nation. These competitions are both in indoor and outdoor games. The institutions work for both curricular and co-curricular development of children.

TEACHER TRAINING

In an attempt to improve the quality and status of teacher, changes were introduced in the early 80s. Teachers for pre-schools and other schools are trained at teacher training schools, pedagogical institutions as well as at the universities.

Teacher Training Schools

Teacher training schools in the category of specialised secondary educational institutions are offering four year course training for teachers for pre schools, for primary grades, teachers of art, music and singing, physical training institutions, vocational training instructors and youth pioneer leaders.

Admission to these teacher training institutes is on the basis of written tests in language, literature and mathematics to ensure subject competency, which is a problem in India as well as U.S.A.

Curriculum of the teacher training school is a combination of content in school subjects and pedagogical theory (including methods and strategies) as well as practice (in teaching). In India, since the primary teacher teaches all subjects, there is no specialization of the subjects.

To impart necessary skills in language, the physical aspects of writing, elocution and expression are included. The other subjects taught to future teacher are music, drawing, physical education and crafts.

Each institution has a demonstration school attached where initially the student teachers observe lessons on a prescribed proforma in the first term and in the second term, the student teacher gives lessons six hrs. per week. In the third term, teaching diminishes and in the fourth and last term, these student teachers work as regular staff of a school.

The examination is state level and has oral, written and practical components.

Students at a teacher training institution are the locals.

Teachers for subjects like music, dance, painting, etc. are trained at such training schools. The course inputs are pedagogy and school teaching.

There are special schools for handicapped (disabled) children where 'special teachers' teach. Separate special training schools for such teachers are also in the category. There are separate admission bonds for these special schools. They are trained either in defectology departments or pedagogical institutes. Teachers are trained to use a variety of sensory materials with children.

Pedagogical Institutes

These 18 university level institutes prepare teachers to teach grades V to X or XI. The duration of the training course is 4-years or 5-years when in a university.

The admission requirement is complete of secondary education. To each at junior secondary level a high school certificate as well as a lower diploma after three years. Teachers of high schools need a degree from university as well as a higher diploma from a pedagogical institute.

As in the U.S. the pedagogical institutes also train teachers for elementary level and kindergartens. Admission to pedagogical institutes is on the basis of tests (as followed in more and more institutes in India to ensure subject competency and aptitude) in Russia language and literature, a foreign language, mathematics and subjects relevant to faculty in which prospective teacher is seeking admission.

Each institute has six to seven faculties which offer a variety of courses the student can select. Pedagogy, comprising psychology, pedagogy, school hygiene and history of pedagogy, is taught in the second year. The teacher training institutes offer courses in socio-economic subjects like political philosophies, political economics and the like as well as special subjects which provide knowledge in the optional field and an acquaintance with modern research techniques.

Correspondence Pedagogical Institutes

The correspondence pedagogical institutes are spread out. Correspondence departments exist in pedagogical institutes, universities and schools and the courses they offer are a year longer than in the formal course.

Education through correspondence courses is popular and several primary level teachers intending to improve qualifications and status and enroll in them. The correspondence and evening courses motivate entry into teaching.

Establishment of resource centres facilitate learning for correspondence students. Considerable encouragement is offered to correspondence students who are working.

University Educational Department: Departments of Education Universities also provide education to teachers. They are merely graduates who are offered pedagogy, psychology and history of pedagogy; practice teaching is done once in the school. The professional input is considered low naturally, but the strengths in the specialization are expected to compensate.

In India, fresh post-graduates are taken in directly by private institutes and some government run Kendriya Vidyalaya.

Academy of Pedagogical Science

The erstwhile USSR Academy of Pedagogical Science has a core faculty with various other types of membership including the best teachers in the country. The affiliation of research institutions in various related areas provides a continuous flow of theoretical and practical knowledge to be tried out and adopted.

The Academy also has a facility for training teacher educations, and publishing facility (Pedagogies Publishing House) so as to disseminate material and develop curricula and textbooks. In fact, it is very similar to the NCERT in India.

In-service Education Programme

Every five years, a school teacher has an opportunity to renew knowledge and competencies as envisaged in the POA, 1986 and the revised POA 1992. The incentive is also the same as in India, which are increments. Within a school as well a teacher has the opportunity to grow and they have to regularly attend.

The programmes have been extended and are of a month's duration—the major ones being longer. Weekend courses/ programmes are also organised for the teachers living within easy reach of the pedagogical centre of which each district has one. Each republic has an in-service training institute. Just as in India the in-service institutes provide opportunity for upgrading knowledge and competencies of teachers, help them solve classroom problems as well aspirations with regards to professional growth so as to keep the fire burning in them. Most of these are naturally at institutes of higher learning. Just like MOST (Massive Orientation of School Teachers), a specific curricula is drawn up, material developed and large numbers of teachers are provided an advanced level of training.

Most of the orientation is through correspondence. Attempt is made to provide inputs relevant to their needs and experiences.

Specific institutes for developing approaches, methods, strategies catering to needs of supervisory staff, school heads and their teachers have also been set up.

CHANGING TRENDS

Changes occurring in the school system structure, curriculum strategies, all require concomitant inputs in teacher education programme.

With the lowering of age of entry into primary school by one year (6 years), the number of years children will remain in school increases. Therefore, the number of teachers required also increase considerably. The need for increased enrolment in teacher training institutes also increases. Proposed changes like reducing class size would also have the same impact.

It is hoped that by reducing class size and increasing teachers' salaries, better potential can be drawn into teaching. To meet the challenges of the electronic age, all teachers need to be made computer literate to enable them to welcome computers in school to assist them and also use them effectively in the learning process. For this, computer training would be needed.

Those desiring industrial participation require greater acquaintance with machines to develop positive attitudes and skills. Therefore, such opportunities are needed in the school curriculum for which general school curriculum is being reorganised.

Teacher education curriculum has to continuously respond to desired changes in any part of the education system.

Evaluate Yourself

1. How is the programme of compulsory school education in Russia different from that in India? What according to you is the purpose of this unique schooling?
2. Why is pre-schooling education gaining province?
3. What is the difference in the role of universities and the academy of pedagogical sciences in teacher education in Russia?

SUMMARY

1. Attendance at school is compulsory for a period of 11-years comprising stay out primary school, incomplete secondary school and vocational, specialised secondary or higher education.

2. Activities termed as extra mutual (co-curricular activities in India) receive significant emphasis.
3. In fact, teacher training for these activities is arranged specifically just as in teacher training schools and pedagogical institutes specific institution and then variety of course, within the institution.
4. Teacher training is considered a job requiring specific abilities therefore careful screening is done at the entry to the training course.
5. Need for continuous development is reflected in the acceptance of in-service education as a regular on-going programme.

KEYWORDS

CPI	=	Correspondence Pedagogical Institutes in Russia
POA	=	Programme of Action
MOST	=	Massive Orientation of School Teachers

MODEL ANSWERS

Specialised Teacher Training Schools. Training schools preparing teachers for special subjects like music dance and painting, etc.

Pedagogical Institute. University level institute which prepares teachers for elementary and Kindergarten level to XI level.

Correspondence Pedagogical Institute. Institute offering education through correspondence. The duration of course is one year longer from the former course.

REFERENCES

Barr, A.S. (1985). Characteristics of Successful Teacher, *Phi, Delta Kappa*, March.

Bhattacharya, G.S. (1990). *Teacher Education*, Vinod Pustak Mandir, Agra, U.P.

Biddle, B.J. and Ellena (1964). *Contemporary Researches on Teachers Education*, Holt Rinehart and Winston, New York.

Dandekar, W.N. (1971). *Evaluation in School*, Sri Vidya Prakashan, Pune.

Davies, I.K. (1971). *The Management of Learning*, McGraw Hill Book Co., London.

Deway, J. (1916). *Democracy and Education*, MacMillan Book Co., New York.

Khan, M.S. (1983). *Teacher Education in India and Abroad*, New Delhi, Ashish Publishing House.

Kolner, James D. (1968). *Reforms in Education*, London, Weldenfield Nicolson.

Shukla, R.S. (1978). *Emerging Trends in Teacher Education*, Chugh Publication, Allahabad.

FURTHER READINGS

Good, C.V. (Ed. 1995). *Dictionary of Education*, McGraw Hill Book Co., New York.

Green, T.F. (1971). *The Activities of Teaching*, McGraw Hill Book Co., New York.

Gupta, A.K. (1998). *Teacher Education*, Sterling Publishers, New Delhi.

Jangira, N.K. (1979). *Teachers' Training and Teachers' Effectiveness: An Experiment in Teacher Behaviour*, National Publishing House, New Delhi.

Kundu, C.L. (1988). *Indian Year Book on Teacher Education*, Sterling Publications, New Delhi.

Passi, B.K. (1976). *Becoming Better Teacher: Micro-teaching Approach*, Sahitya Mudranalaya, Ahmedabad.

Saxena, N.R., Mishra, B.K. and Mohanty, R.K. (1998). *Teacher Education*, R. Lall Book Depot, Meerut.

Sharma, R.A. (2002). *Teacher Education*, International Publishing House, Meerut (U.P.).

Shukla, R.S. (1989). *Shikshak Shiksha: Dasha Evam Disha* (in Hindi) Akshat Prakashan, Udaipur, Rajasthan.

Tibble, J.W. (1971). *Future of Teacher Education*, Routledge and Kegan Paul, London.

LEARNING EXERCISE

1. Discuss the general aims and objectives of teacher education programme.

2. "Teaching practice is an essential component of teacher education programme". In the light of this statement, explain the principles and objectives of organising teaching practice.
3. What are the recent trends in education? Explain any one model.
4. Critically examine the activities of NCTE for in-service education of teachers.
5. Compare and contrast the teacher education programme in U.K. and U.S.A.
6. How will you evaluate the effectiveness of teacher education programme?
7. Explain the various principles involved in formulating a curricular programme for teachers.
8. What do you mean by professionalisation of teacher education programme.
9. Explain the need and importance of professional organisation of teacher education.
10. Analyse the teacher education programme in a democratic society.

Bibliography

Adaval, S.E. (1984). *Analytical Study of Teacher Education in India*, Allabahad: Amitabh Prakashan.

Agarwal, J.C. (1988). *New Education Policy—1986*, Delhi: Prabhat Prakashan.

Allen, D.W. (1966). *Micro-teaching: A Description*, Stanford University, California (Mimeo).

Allen, D.W. and Ryan, K.A. and Allen, W.H. (1960). *Micro-teaching, Reading*, Addison-Wesley, Massachusetts.

Amidon, E.J. and Flanders, N.A. (1963). The Role of the Teacher in the Classroom: A Manual for Understanding and Improving Teachers Classroom Behaviour, Amidon and Associates, Minneapolis.

Amidon, E.J. and Hough, J. (1967). Interaction Analysis: Theory, Research and Application, Reading, Massachusetts: Addison-Wesley Publishing Co., Inc.

Anderson, R.C. and Faust, G.W. (1973). *Educational Psychology: The Science of Instruction and Learning*. New York: Dodd-Mean & Co.

Argyle, M. (1972). *The Psychology of Interpersonal Behaviour*, Harmondsworth, Penguin.

Ausubel, D.P. (1963). *The Psychology of Meaningful Verbal Learning*, New York: Grunne and Stratton.

Ausubel, D.P. (1968). *Educational Psychology: A Cognitive View*, New York: Holt, Rinehart & Winston, Inc.

Barnard, H.C. (1967). *An Introduction to Teaching*, London: University of London Press.

Barr, A.S. (1985). Characteristics of Successful Teachers, *Phi Delta Kappa*, March.

Bellack, A.A. et. al. (1966). *The Language of Classroom.* Columbia: Teachers' College Press.

Bennett, R.V. (1973). Organising Strategies, Classroom Interaction Patterns and Pupil Affect, *Journal of Educational Research*, Vol. 66, May, pp. 381-93.

Bennett, W.A. (1969). The Language Laboratory in Higher Education (in D. Unwin Ed.), *Media and Methods of Instructional Technology of Higher Education*, London: McGraw Hill Book Co.

Bentley, E.L. and Miller, E. (1971). Equivalent Talk Categories, (in R.L. Ober, E.L. Bentley and E. Miller), *Systematic Observation of Teaching*, New Jersey: Prentice-Hall Inc.

Bernard, H.W. (1965). *Psychology of Learning and Teaching*, New York: McGraw Hill Book Co.

Best, J.W. (1959). *Research in Education*, New Jersey: Prentice Hall, Englewood Cliffs.

Best, J.W. (1977). *Research in Education* (3rd Edition), New Jersey: Prentice-Hall, Englewood Cliffs.

Bhargava, M. (1978). *Modern Psychological Testing and Measurement* (in Hindi), Agra: Harprasad & Sons.

Bhattacharya, G.C. (1984). Effectiveness of Various Models of Teaching Geography in Relation to Institutional Resources, Ph.D. Thesis, Education, B.H.U., Varanasi.

Bhattacharya G.C. (1979). Effectiveness of Diode Model of Integration in the Acquisition of Teaching Skills and Attitude of student Teachers Towards Teaching, Unpublished M.Ed., Dissertation, B.H.U., Varanasi.

Biddle, B.J. and Elena (1964). *Contemporary Researches on Teacher Effectiveness*, New York: Holt, Rinchart and Winston.

Bloom, B.S. (1956). *Taxonomy of Educational Objectives: Cognitive Domain* (Book-I), New York: McKay.

Bloom, B.S. (1963). Historical Examples of Teaching Methods (in N.L. Gage (Ed.)), *Handbook of Research on Teaching*, Chicago: Rand, McNally & Co.

Bradfield, J.M. and Moredock, H.S. (1975). Measurement and Evaluation in Education in M. Bhargava: *Modern Psychological Testing and Measurement* (in Hindi), Agra: Harprasad Bhargava.

Bruner, J. (1966). *Towards a Theory of Instruction*, New York: Norton Co.

——— (1969). The Functions of Teaching (in Frey and Haugen (Ed.)). *Readings in Classroom Learning*, New York: Van Nostrand Reinhold & Co.

Bruner, J., Goodnow, J.J. and Austin, G.A. (1967). *A Study of Thinking*, New York: Science Editions Inc.

Buch, M.B. (Ed. 1974). Survey of Research in Education, Centre of Advanced Study in Education, Vadodara: M.S. University of Baroda.

Buch, M.B. and Sanathanan, S.R. (1970). Communication in Classroom, CASE, Vadodara: M.S.U. of Baroda.

Burton, K. (1979). Teaching-Learning Process (in S.S. Chauhan), *Innovations in Teaching-Learning Process*, New Delhi: Vikash Publishing House (Pvt.) Ltd.

Challenges of Education Policy Perspective (1985). Ministry of Human Resource Development, New Delhi: Govt. of India.

Clark, C.M. (1979). Five Faces of Research of Teaching, Educational Leadership, Vol. 37. No. 1, pp. 29-31.

Clarke, S.C.T. (1970). A General Teaching Theory. *The Journal of Teacher Education*, Vol. XXI, No. 3, Fall.

Cleary, A., Mayes, T. and Packham, D. (1976). *Educational Technology: Implications for Early and Special Education*, London: John Wiley and Sons.

Combs, A.W. (1964). The Personal Approach to Good Teaching, *Educational Leadership*, Vol. 21, No. 6, March.

Compbell, D.T. and Stanley, J.C. (1965). Experimental and Quasi-experimental Designs for Research on Teaching (in N.L. Gage Ed.), *Handbook of Research on Teaching*, Chicago: Rand McNally & Co.

Crawford, M.P. (1963). Concepts of Training (in R.M. Gagne (Ed.)), *Psychological Principles in System Development*, Holt, New York: Rinehart and Winston.

Crowder, N.A. (1959). Automatic Tutoring by Means of Intrinsic Programming in E.H. Galanter (Ed.) *Automatic Teaching: The State of the Art*, New York: Wiley.

Cruickshank, D.R. Simulation: New Direction in Teacher Preparation, *Phi Delta Kappa*, Vol. 48, No. 1.

Dandekar, W.N. (1971). *Evaluation in Schools*, Poona: Shri Vidya Pakashan.

Das, R.C., Passi, B.K. and Singh, L.C. (1980). *Differential Effectiveness of Micro-teaching Components*, NCERT, Sri Aurobindo Marg, New Delhi.

Davies, I.K. (1971). Developing Accountability in Instructional Systems Technology (in D. Packham, A. Cleary and T. Mayes (Eds.)), *Aspects of Educational Technology-V*, London: Pitman.

———. (1971). Presentation Strategies in Programmed Learning, (in J. Harley (Ed.)), *Programmed Learning and Educational Technology*, London: Illiffc.

———. (1971). *The Management of Learning*, London: McGraw Hill Book Co.

DeCecco, J.P. (1968). *The Psychology of Learning and Instruction*, Prentice Hall Inc., New Jersey: Englewood Cliffs.

DeCecco, J.P. and Crawford, W.R. (1977). *The Psychology of Learning and Instruction: Educational Technology*, New Delhi: Prentice Hall of India.

Desai, D.B. et al. (Eds. (1980)). Researches in Classrooms, Monograph, Vadodara: CASE M.S.U. of Baroda.

Deway, J. (1916). *Democracy and Education*, New York: MacMillan Book Co.

Dixit, U.N. (1980). A Comparative Study of the Effects of Varying Sources of Feedback Upon the GTC among the Student Teachers (in *Differential Effectiveness of Microteaching Components*, NCERT, Sr Aurobindo Marg, New Delhi).

Evans, M.N. (1971). Functional Patterns of K.G. Teachers by Interaction Analysis. Dissttn. Abstr. Int. 31.1 5902 A.

Flanders, N.A. (1960). *Teacher Influence, Pupil Attitudes and Achievement*, University of Minnesota, Minneapolis.

———. (1970). *Analysing Teaching Behaviour, Reading*, Massachusetts: Addison Wesley Publishing Co., Inc.

Gage, N.L. (1963). Paradigms for Research on Teaching (in N. Gage (Ed.)), *Handbook of Research on Teacher Rand*, Chicago: McNally & Co.

——— (1967). Psychological Conceptions of Teaching, *Inter. Jl of Edul. Sr.*, Vol. I, pp. 151-61.

——— (Ed. 1965). *Handbook of Research on Teaching*, Chicago: Rand McNally & Co.

Gagne, R.M. (1963). *The Conditions of Learning*, New York: Holt Rinchart & Winston Inc.

——— (1965). Simulators (in R. Glaser (Ed.)), Training, Research and Education, New York: John Wiley.

——— (1966). The Learning of Principles (in H.J. Klausmeier and C.W. Harris (Eds.)), *Analysis of Concept Learning*, Academic Press Inc., New York.

Gandhi, P. (1981). Academic Achievement in Relation to Achievement Motive, Affiliation Motive and Power Motive, Unpublished Ph.D., Thesis, Education, B.H.U., Varanasi.

Glaser, R. (1962). Psychology and Instructional Technology, in R. Glaser (Ed.), *Training Research and Education*, Pittsburgh: University of Pittsburgh Press.

———. (1963). Instructional Technology and Measurement of Outcome: Some Questions, *American Psychologists*, Vol. 18.

Glasser, R. and Nitco, A.J. (1971). Measurement in Learning and Instruction (in R.L. Thorndike (Ed.)), *Educational*

Measurement, 2nd Ed., American Council of Education, Washington D.C.

Glasser, W. (1965). Reality Therapy, New York. Harper and Row.

Glatter, R. and Wedell, E.H. (1971). *Study by Correspondence*, London: Longmans.

Good, C.V. (Ed. 1995). *Dictionary of Education*, New York: McGraw Hill Book Co.

Green, B.A. Jr. (1974). *The Personalised System of Instruction*, Washington, D.C.

Green, T.F. (1971). *The Activities of Teaching*, New York: McGraw Hill Book Co.

Grondlund, N.E. (1970). *Stating Behavioural Objectives for Classroom Instruction*, London: MacMillan Co.

Gupta, A.K. (1988). *Teacher Education*, New Delhi: Sterling Publishers.

Gupta, V.P. and Dutta, R. (1984). A Comparative Study of Effectiveness of Micro-Teaching under simulated conditions and Micro-teaching with varying class size upon the GTC and change in Anxiety Level, in *Relative Effectiveness of Variation in Microteaching Component*, NTE, NCERT, Sri Aurobindo Marg, New Delhi.

Hargie, O.D.W. and Maidment, P.A. (1978). Discrimination Training and Micro-teaching: Implications for Teaching Practice, *British Jl. of Edl. Technology*, Vol. 2, No. 9, pp. 87-93.

Hargie, O.P.W., Dickson, D.A. and Tittmar, H.D. (1978): Miniteaching—An Extension of the Micro-teaching Format, *British Jl. of Teacher Education*, Vol. 4, No. 2, pp. 113-18.

Hebb, D.O. (1966). *A Text-book of Psychology*, W.B. Saunders Co., Phidelphia.

Herbart, J.F. (1904). *Outlines of Educational Doctrine*, New York: MacMillan Book Co.

Herry, A. Ober Street (1929). Panel Discussion (in R.A. Sharma), *Teacher Education*, Meerut: International Pub. House.

Hilgard, E.R. and Bower, G.H. (1975). *Theories of Learning*, New Jersey: Prentice Hall Inc., Englewood Cliffs.

Hough, J.B. and Duncan, J.K. (1970). *Teaching: Description and Analysis*. California: Addison-Wesley.

Hunt, D.E. and Sullivan, E.V. (1974). *Between Psychology and Education*. Illinois: The Dryden Press.

Hyman, R.T. (1967). Teaching: Triadic and Dynamics, *The Educational Forum*, Vol. 32, November.

Jangira, N.K. (1979). *Teachers' Training and Teachers' Effectiveness: An Experiment in Teacher Behaviour*, New Delhi: National Publishing House.

———. (1983). *Technology of Classroom Questioning*, New Delhi: National Publishing House.

Joyce, B. and Weil, M. (1972). *Models of Teaching*, New Jersey: Prentice Hall Inc., Englewood Cliffs.

Joyco, B.R. (1975). Teaching Strategies for Learning Centre, *Educational Leadership*, Vol. 32, No. 6, pp. 388-91.

Kellar, F.S. (1974). *Ten Years of Personalised Instruction*, *Teaching of Psychology*, October.

Kersh, B.Y. (1961). The Classroom Simulator: An Audio-Visual Environment for Practice Teaching, *Audio-Visual Instruction*, Vol. 6.

Kilpatrick, W.H. (1963). *How We Learn*, Calcutta: YMCA Publishing House.

Koran, J.J. (1971). Supervision: An Attempt to Modify Behaviour, *Educational Leadership*, Vol. 26, pp. 759-67.

Krathwohl, D.R., Bloom, B.S. and Masia, B.B. (1964). *Taxonomy of Educational Objectives: Handbook-II: Affective Domain*, New York: McKay.

Kulshrestha, S.P. (1979). *Mini-teaching: A New Experiment in Teacher Education*, Research Monograph, Dehradoon.

Kundu, C.L. (1988). *Indian Year-book on Teacher Education*, New Delhi: Sterling Publications.

Mehta, C.S. and Joshi, D.C. (1973). *Principles and Problems of Teacher Education*, Pt. I and II (in Hindi), Jaipur: Rajasthan Hindi Grantha Academy.

Morrison, A. and McIntyra, D. (1969). *Teacher and Teaching*, Armondsworth, Penguin.

Morrison, H.C. (1984). *Basic Principles of Education*, Boston: Houton-Miffin.

Nicholas, R.C. and Davis, J.A. (1964). Characteristics of Students of High Academic Aptitudes, *Personnel Guide, Jl.*, Vol. 42, pp. 794-800.

Ober, R.L. (1971). Predicting the Verbal Behaviour of Students from Data Collected During Student Teaching (in R.L. Ober, et al.)) *Systematic Observation of Teaching*, New Jersey: Englewood Cliffs.

Ober, R.L., Bentley, E.L. and Miller, E. (1971). *Systematic Observation of Teaching*, Prentice Hall Inc., New Jersey: Englewood Cliffs.

Palsane, M.N. and Gandhi, D. (1967). *Practice Teaching, Teacher Education*, Vol. 1, No. 3, pp. 1-37.

Pangotra, N.N. (1972). A Study of the Effects of Feedback from Different Sources on the Classroom Behaviour of Student Teachers Using the Technique of Interaction Analysis, Unpublished Ph.D. Thesis, Education, Vadodara: M.S. University of Baroda.

Passi, B.K. (1976). Becoming Better Teacher: Micro-teaching Approach, Ahmedabad: Sahitya Mudranalaya.

———. (1974). *Micro-teaching in Teacher Education*, CASE. Vadodara: M.S. University of Baroda.

Patterson, C.H. (1977). *Foundations for a Theory of Instruction and Educational Psychology*, New York: Harper & Row.

Reid, R.L. (1969). Educational Technology: The Background and Need (in D. Unwin), *Media and Methods*, New York: McGraw Hill Book Co.

Remmers, H.H. and Gage, N.L. (1955). *Educational Measurement and Evaluation*, New York: Harper and Brothers.

Remmers, H.H. Gage, N.L. and Rummel (1985). *A Practical Introduction to Measurement and Evaluation*, Delhi: Universal Book Stall.

Report (1953): Report of the Secondary Education Commission, Ministry of Education and Social Welfare, Govt. of India New Delhi.

——— (1964): Internship in Teaching, NCERT Publication, NCERT, Sri Aurobindo Marg, New Delhi.

——— (1966): Report of the Education Commission: Education for National Development (1964-66), Ministry of Education, Govt. of India, New Delhi.

——— (1986): Programme of Action: New Education Policy, Ministry of Human Resource Development, Govt. of India, New Delhi.

——— (1986): Report of the Working Groups on In-service Education of Teachers, NCERT, Sri Aurobindo Marg, New Delhi.

Resource Book on Teacher Education: NCERT Publication, NCERT, Sri Aurobindo Marg, New Delhi.

Robb, C. (1973). Notes on the Systems Approach to Management, Administrative Staff College, Henley, April.

Russeli, D.H. (1960). Teaching for Concept Development (in C.W. Harris (Ed.)). *Encyclopedia of Educational Research*, New York: The MacMillan Co.

Ryan, D.G. (1960). Characteristics of Teachers, Their Description, Comparison and Appraisal: A Research Study, American Council on Education, Washington, D.C.

Ryan, D.G. (1963). Assessment of Teacher Behaviour and Instruction, *Review of Educational Research*, Vol. 33, pp. 415-47.